the devoted mind

"I thirst."
JOHN 19:28

the
devoted
mind

Seeking God's Face
in a World of Distraction

Kris Lundgaard

P U B L I S H I N G
P.O. BOX 817 • PHILLIPSBURG • NEW JERSEY 08865-0817

Unless otherwise noted, all Scripture quotations are from the New King James Version®. Copyright © 1982 by Thomas Nelson. Used by permission. All rights reserved.

Scripture quotations marked (ESV) are from the ESV® Bible (The Holy Bible, English Standard Version®), copyright © 2001 by Crossway, a publishing ministry of Good News Publishers. Used by permission. All rights reserved.

Scripture quotations marked (NIV) are from the Holy Bible, New International Version®, NIV®. Copyright © 1973, 1978, 1984, 2011 by Biblica, Inc.™ Used by permission of Zondervan. All rights reserved worldwide. www.zondervan.com. The "NIV" and "New International Version" are trademarks registered in the United States Patent and Trademark Office by Biblica, Inc.™

Scripture quotations marked (NLT) are from the *Holy Bible*, New Living Translation, copyright © 1996, 2004, 2015 by Tyndale House Foundation. Used by permission of Tyndale House Publishers, Inc., Carol Stream, Illinois 60188. All rights reserved.

Italics within Scripture quotations indicate emphasis added.

Drawing of The Cruciform Tree *by Lenka Knoetze*
Cover design by Jelena Mirkovic

ISBN: 978-1-62995-968-9 (pbk)
ISBN: 978-1-62995-969-6 (ePub)

Printed in the United States of America

Library of Congress Cataloging-in-Publication Data has been applied for.

To
my son Kristian Augustine,
whose heart finds rest in God,

and

in memoriam
J. I. Packer,
my teacher

Let the hearts of those rejoice who seek the LORD!
Seek the LORD and His strength;
Seek His face evermore!
—PSALM 105:3–4

Teach me to seek thee,
and reveal thyself to me, when I seek thee,
for I cannot seek thee, except thou teach me,
nor find thee, except thou reveal thyself.
Let me seek thee in longing,
let me long for thee in seeking;
let me find thee in love,
and love thee in finding.
—ANSELM OF CANTERBURY

Contents

Preface

our nearest approach to heaven in this world

He often visiteth our Minds,
But cold Acceptance in us ever finds:
We send Him often griev'd away:
Else would He shew us all His Kingdom's Joy.
—THOMAS TRAHERNE

All his kingdom's joy? That would be something to know about. And what is all his kingdom's joy but to know him and to have him? But how can our cold minds extend God warm welcome and taste his joy—not in eternity but in this troubled and troubling world? That's what I'd like to know, and I believe a seventeenth-century pastor's deathbed devotions can help.

Age and sickness had left John Owen "every way unable to do any thing for the edification of others." Convinced that he would never return to public ministry, he wrote out his meditations. His

1. John Owen, *The Grace and Duty of Being Spiritually Minded*, 1681, in *The Works of John Owen*, ed. William H. Goold, 24 vols. (Edinburgh: Johnstone & Hunter, 1850–1855; reprint by Banner of Truth Trust, 1965, 1991), 7:263.

theme was Paul's blessing on the devoted mind: "To be spiritually minded is life and peace" (Rom. 8:6). No doubt the shadow of death sharpened his hunger for that promise. But when God later healed him, Owen turned those devotions into what he called a "small and plain discourse" for all our cold and captive minds.[2]

In it Owen explains why he thinks his book is well timed: He finds the world fervent "to impose itself on the minds of men," armed with the means to possess those minds. If the world catches people's thoughts, it will have their longings too, he warns. When this happens, even believers are hardened against faithfully following Christ, and they begin to "walk and talk as if the world were all" and to grow distracted, despondent, weary, and unresponsive to God's grace.[3] But the spiritual mind has hope: its unwandering focus on Christ and heavenly things yields life and peace, the "*nearest approaches unto heaven and blessedness*" we can reach in this world.[4]

In the centuries since Owen wrote, the world has multiplied its means to trap our minds and cool our hearts. But he can still help us—if we can overcome the barrier of the *way* he wrote to reach the treasure of *what* he wrote. Owen's writing style is infamously intimidating, but his content is famously worth the trouble. J. I. Packer explained that "on first reading he tires the mind quite quickly," but if you press on to a third reading, by then you "should be able to grasp Owen's vision of the awesome beauty of God's ways."[5]

The awesome beauty of God's ways. That's where our minds belong, where he'll "shew us all His Kingdom's Joy." So for every cold and captive mind, mine included, I've adapted Owen's

2. Owen, 7:263.

3. Owen, 7:264, 496.

4. Owen, 7:497; italics his.

5. J. I. Packer, "John Owen on Spiritual-Mindedness," *Banner of Truth* 620 (May 2015), 15.

discourse in a way that I hope overcomes the barrier and opens a door to his exposition of what it means for us to seek God's face always.[6]

Three Motifs

One way I have represented Owen's teaching is through three themes or motifs: *the devoted mind, the seeking of God's face,* and *the Beloved.* These are scattered through Owen's book and expressed differently, but I've made them prominent. Together they focus and flavor my version of Owen's all-encompassing approach to spiritual mindedness.

By *devoted* I mean a mind set apart for the Lord (Lev. 27:28), a mind completely given over to him and to his service (2 Chron. 31:4; 1 Cor. 16:15). I also use *devoted* to suggest a lover whose full attention has been captured by her Beloved, to whom she offers all her powers (Song 2:14, 16; 6:3; 7:10; 8:6–7), whose devotion is expressed by the hymn "Take My Life, and Let It Be."[7]

By *the seeking of God's face,* I mean the pursuit of his intimate presence, a sense of closeness, a clearer and deeper personal knowledge of him, and an assurance of his acceptance, love, and blessing. We are finding our way back to the intimacy of Eden, a journey now possible in Christ who is the "new and living Way" into God's holy presence (Heb. 10:20). Of course we won't fully realize this intimacy until we see Christ face-to-face in eternity, yet we taste it now and pursue as much of him as we can have on earth (Ps. 27:8). And as we draw near to God, he draws near to us (James 4:8).

6. For those who'd like to read Owen in his own words, yet gracefully abridged and modernized, I recommend R. J. K. Law's *Spiritual-Mindedness* (Carlisle, PA: Banner of Truth Trust, 2009). Law sticks to the script; I color outside the lines.
7. Frances R. Havergal, 1874.

I often use *Beloved* to name our Triune God or Christ himself. He is the object of the devoted mind—not in an academic sense but as the ultimate object of our desire, the One whose presence we seek. God has made the love, commitment, and intimacy of marriage the crowning image of his relationship to his people, so he is properly our Beloved (Song 8:6; Mark 2:18–20; 2 Cor. 11:2; Eph. 5:29–32).

Let these three motifs remind you that the purpose of spiritual mindedness is communion with God.

The End of Each Chapter

By the "end" of each chapter, I mean two things: First, I mean what comes last. What comes last in each chapter is a section called "Reflection and Praxis." You may be tempted to skip it. But it isn't a set of exercises for overachievers; it's meant to guide the real mind-work and heart-work of consolidating the ideas of the chapter where they must be consolidated: in our prayers and meditations, in our worship and conversation, in our contemplation of God and communion with Christ. Even if you don't have time to do the suggested work when you read the chapter, reading through the exercises will extend some of your thinking about the chapter, and you can decide whether to come back to some of them later. I also use this section to suggest further reading for several of the chapters.

By the "end" of each chapter, I also mean its purpose. The purpose of each chapter is to draw our attention to our Beloved but not to admire him from a distance. Whether this end of each chapter is achieved is between you and God. You may draw close to him, or you may keep a safe distance. Reflecting on and practicing the content of each chapter is meant to help you draw close.

A Personal Note

I've rewritten John Owen's exposition of spiritual mind-edness, which he wrote from the depth of his long experience with God. I don't mean to take credit for his spiritual maturity and nearness to God any more than I mean to take credit for his insights. Rewriting his work, much more than reading it, has made clear to me how far I have yet to go. Therefore, may the Spirit grant *us* the grace to devote our minds to Christ our Beloved, to always seek the face of the one who himself is our life and peace.

Introduction

the devoted mind

O God, You are my God;
Early will I seek You;
My soul thirsts for You;
My flesh longs for You
In a dry and thirsty land
Where there is no water.
—PSALM 63:1

The Great Thirst

Father Latour was lost. His canteen was empty. Fever in his mouth sickened him; dizziness unsettled him. The repeated shapes of the hills and junipers of the New Mexican desert made him feel he was "wandering in some geometrical nightmare." He closed his eyes to clear his head.

When he opened his eyes again, his glance immediately fell upon one juniper which differed in shape from the others. It was not a thick-growing cone, but a naked, twisted trunk, perhaps ten feet high, and at the top it parted into two lateral, flat-lying branches, with a little crest of green in the centre, just above the cleavage. Living vegetation could not present more faithfully the form of the Cross.

The traveller dismounted, drew from his pocket a much worn book, and baring his head, knelt at the foot of the cruciform tree.[1]

In his own wasting thirst, he remembered "that cry, wrung from his Saviour on the Cross, *J'ai soif!* Of all our Lord's physical sufferings, only one, 'I thirst,' rose to His lips."[2] Latour's own thirst was redirected to the Living Water, to communion with his Beloved.

Here was a man whose only hope for life on this earth was water. What could make him, while he still had strength, delay his desperate search?

A greater thirst.

With his mind so keen on Christ that it resists his body's self-preserving reflexes, Latour is an emblem, a symbol, of the devoted mind that finds life and peace. As an emblem, he embodies the thirst for communion with God in Christ that we will explore, a thirst never slaked. That thirst is born when God's Spirit recreates us; it grows stronger the more we taste of heavenly things. A spiritual mind takes hold of heaven, of Christ, of God, and won't let go. Such a mind knows that nothing else will satisfy, so it methodically lays aside every distraction for the sake of the One Thing Needed (Luke 10:42).

Paul sets such a mind apart.

The Great Comma

For to be carnally minded is death,
but to be spiritually minded is life and peace. (Rom. 8:6)

1. Willa Cather, *Death Comes for the Archbishop*, in *Later Novels*, ed. Sharon O'Brien (New York: Library of America, 1990), 286.
2. Cather, 287; see John 19:28.

The two halves of Romans 8:6 are separated by a comma. On the page the comma looks small, but the gap it represents could swallow galaxies. No one lives in the gap; no one straddles the gap; the gap categorically divides humanity with a double dichotomy.

The first dichotomy is between two dispositions of the mind: *fleshly*[3] or *spiritual*. Paul doesn't suggest a spectrum, a more-or-lessness. He states a stark either/or: either a mind is given over to the flesh, or it is devoted to the Spirit. The second dichotomy is equally exclusive: *death* or *life and peace*. Paul contrasts in a few words the misery of those who are fleshly minded with the happiness of those who are spiritually minded. The fleshly minded taste death now and, apart from God's saving grace in Christ, will endure eternal death; the spiritually minded taste life and peace now, and thanks to saving grace they will forever drink life and peace.

You might object that this is too black-and-white. You know that not even the godliest believers have their minds always on things of the Spirit, and you know unbelievers whose minds aren't always consumed by the flesh. We'll soon see that Paul agrees with you. But for now, we'll let the fork in Paul's road goad us. Let it prod us to confirm that we're on the life-and-peace side of the Great Comma. Let it kindle an urgency not only to understand what spiritual mindedness is but by grace to get and guard it.[4]

Paul's dichotomy notwithstanding, we know that no believer's mind is completely and continuously spiritual. Paul says as much

---

3. The NKJV translates forms of *sarx* as "flesh" for the noun and "carnal" and "carnally" for adjective and adverb. Except when quoting the NKJV I will stick with forms of "flesh" for the sake of style. There is no difference in meaning.

4. The title of Owen's book is illuminating: *The Grace and Duty of Being Spiritually Minded*. Grace is the work of God's Spirit in us, and it is compatible with our obedience. In fact, by grace the Spirit recreates us; grace makes possible and calls forth our response to God. Grace and duty are therefore united by the gospel. What God has joined together, let no one separate.

when he tells the Galatian believers that "the flesh lusts against the Spirit, and the Spirit against the flesh; and these are contrary to one another, so that you do not do the things that you wish" (Gal. 5:17). Our own experience confirms this aggravating fact of the Christian life. Even Paul faced the same struggle.[5] And as for unbelievers, those on the other side of the Great Comma, God's common grace restrains even his enemies from nonstop evil.[6]

But our inconsistencies and inconstancy don't blur Paul's stark division between the fleshly minded and the spiritually minded. Though we waver, each of us has a spiritual bias; we are either dominated by thoughts and longings that lead to death or devoted to those that lead to life and peace. And these biases are rooted in our identity, in our relation to Christ.

Paul defines the two possible identities in terms of *flesh* and *Spirit*. Those on the death side of the Great Comma are "in the flesh," and those on the life-and-peace side are "in the Spirit" (Rom. 8:9). Note how Paul characterizes these two classes in Roman 8: those in the flesh

- "walk according to the flesh" (v. 4),
- "live according to the flesh" (v. 5),
- "set their minds on the things of the flesh" (v. 5),
- have a mind that is "enmity against God," that does not and cannot subject itself to God's law (v. 7), and
- "cannot please God" (v. 8).

5. See Romans 7:13–25. For a defense of the classical understanding of these verses as a description of the Christian's struggle, see J. I. Packer, "The 'Wretched Man' in Romans 7," in the appendix to *Keep in Step with the Spirit* (Leicester: Inter-Varsity, 1984), 263–70.

6. "Common grace" is God's work in both believers and unbelievers. It bears fruit in our lives and brings God's blessings. But it isn't *saving* grace. See Louis Berkhof, *Systematic Theology*, fourth revised and enlarged edition (Grand Rapids: Eerdmans, 1939, 1941), 432–46; note especially section 2, "The Restraint of Sin," 442.

Paul explains that this is because they do not "have the Spirit of Christ" and therefore are "not his" (v. 9). In Galatians 5:19–21, he describes the unholy outworking of this fleshly mindset:

> Now the works of the flesh are evident, which are: adultery, fornication, uncleanness, lewdness, idolatry, sorcery, hatred, contentions, jealousies, outbursts of wrath, selfish ambitions, dissensions, heresies, envy, murders, drunkenness, revelries, and the like.

Such a person is outside Christ and "will not inherit the kingdom of God" (v. 21).

But in Romans 8, Paul writes that those in the Spirit

- "walk . . . according to the Spirit" (v. 4),
- "live according to the Spirit" (v. 5), and
- "set their minds . . . on the things of the Spirit" (v. 5).

In fact, "the Spirit of God dwells in" them and they have "the Spirit of Christ" (v. 9), which orients their hearts to things of the Spirit. They bear the fruit of the Spirit, which is "love, joy, peace, longsuffering, kindness, goodness, faithfulness, gentleness, self-control" (Gal. 5:22–23).

So there are two kinds of people, one on each side of the Great Comma of Romans 8:6. Those with their minds set on the flesh are spiritually dead now (Eph. 2:1–3; Col. 2:13). Unless they believe in Christ and are born of the Spirit, they will eventually face God's judgment and eternal death: "For if you live according to the flesh you will die" (Rom. 8:13). It can't be otherwise, because, as Paul says, those in the flesh are hostile to God.

On the other side of the Great Comma are those who are in Christ, the spiritually minded who already have life and peace but who can grow in spiritual mindedness. By that growth, they taste more life and enjoy more peace.

This book is about what it means to be spiritually minded, how we grow in spiritual mindedness, and what fruit of spiritual mindedness we can expect to enjoy.

Spiritual mindedness begins with the Holy Spirit.

The Person and Work of the Spirit

The New Testament writers sometimes use the word *spirit* to refer to the *person* of the Holy Spirit and sometimes to the *work* of the Spirit in believers to bring about the life of God in them. It's not always obvious which they mean. Jesus used the word in both senses when he told Nicodemus, "That which is born of the Spirit is spirit" (John 3:6). In other words, those who are born from above by the power of the Holy Spirit live new spiritual lives empowered by the person of the Spirit in them.

Throughout Romans 8, Paul uses the word *spirit* in these two ways as well. For example, he speaks of the *person* of the Spirit in verse 9 as the "Spirit of God" and the "Spirit of Christ." Likewise, in verse 11 he mentions "the Spirit of Him who raised Jesus from the dead." Paul teaches us that we have the Holy Spirit to thank for all the rich benefits that we'll explore.

But in verses 4 and 5, Paul sets walking and living "according to the Spirit" against walking and living "according to the flesh." The flesh is the corrupted principle we are born with, the engine of our sin. Paul contrasts this with the new principle of life the Holy Spirit plants and cultivates in us, the *work* of the Spirit, which is the engine of our loving obedience—of walking and living "according to the Spirit."

Mind-Work in the Spirit

My theme is one aspect of this life in the Spirit—the work and disposition of the mind in Romans 8:5–6. Translations of verse 5 render it to "set [our] minds on the things of the Spirit" (esv), to have our "minds set on what the Spirit desires" (niv), or to "think about things that please the Spirit" (nlt). All of these convey the idea that this is work for our minds, but in so few words it's easy to miss the fullness of that mind-work. The mind-work here isn't limited to the kind of effort needed to memorize the Gettysburg Address or to solve a system of linear equations, as demanding as those tasks can be. The mind-work Paul calls us to demands more than notions and reasoning and memory, though it certainly includes them.

The Greek words behind our translations of *mind* and *mindedness* in Romans 8 convey a fully rounded sense of the work that includes not only knowledge, understanding, wisdom, and discretion but delight. In a related text, Paul says to "set your mind on things above" (Col. 3:2), calling us not only to concentrate and focus our attention but to yearn. The spiritual mind tenaciously clings to its object, relishes it, finds satisfaction in it, cleaves to it, glories in it. Paul portrays a mind unreservedly devoted to its object; he portrays the *devoted mind*.

Love-Work of the Mind

Romantic love, if we can believe the poets, is quasi-religious. The lover is progressively captivated by his beloved in a devotion analogous to the spiritual mindedness that brings life and peace. We can think of the work of a lover's mind—and the work of the mind set on the Spirit—as devotion, and we can think of that devotion in three acts: *contemplation*, *inclination*, and *satisfaction*.

Contemplation

Ubi amor, ibi oculus: "Where love is, there is the eye." The lover turns his eye to his beloved and compares her to a summer's day or a red, red rose. His mind scours all that is good in nature as he looks for images to help him to describe and enjoy her beauty. The spiritual mind likewise turns to God and compares him to a rock, a shepherd, or unapproachable light but finds in those comparisons only shadows, for he is beyond compare. The devoted mind exalts the Beloved above the gods and the creatures of highest heaven. It pores over God's words, God's wisdom, God's ways—everything that will reveal him more clearly. The spiritual mind is devoted and can't be satisfied with a glance but must gaze, muse, meditate. And this gaze isn't distant and detached; by the Spirit the lover approaches God to behold him in his sanctuary (Ps. 63:2; Eph. 2:18).

Inclination

When Solomon dedicates the temple in 1 Kings 8, he asks God to "incline our hearts to Himself" (v. 58). God answers that prayer when we consider him and his ways with minds renewed by the Spirit. Our hearts are softened and warmed by the beauty, majesty, and glory we see in him, and our affections are stirred so that we lean toward our Beloved and long for him "as the deer pants for the water brooks" (Ps. 42:1). Contemplation whets the mind's appetite and keeps it sharp. But the heart inclined toward God closes the distance in eager approach.

Satisfaction

Possessing and relishing the Beloved, the devoted mind acquires a palate trained by the Spirit: God and heavenly things become savory. This is the satisfaction and joy of spiritual life. Mere notions about God are a mouthful of lukewarm water. But the devoted mind drinks the love of Christ, declares it the best wine, and rejoices "with joy inexpressible and full of glory" (1 Peter 1:8).

These three acts follow a natural progression: contemplation (mind-work) leads to inclination and satisfaction (heart-work). Our hearts follow whatever captivates our minds.

Come Away

Is it hard to imagine your mind being as fixed on Jesus as Latour's in the desert? Such devotion often feels like a fantasy to me. Yet Paul doesn't say the spiritual mind is a rare, exclusive prize for elite saints; it is the reality promised to all in Christ; it is Life and Peace. So we thirst, and our Beloved calls: "Rise up, my love, my fair one, and come away" (Song 2:10). Throughout the following chapters, we'll rise and move toward our Beloved. We'll explore the meaning and practice of the love-work of the devoted mind. Our souls "shall be satisfied as with marrow and fatness" (Ps. 63:5).

As we go, we'll attend to the three acts of devotion. In part 1, we'll explore the *contemplation* of the devoted mind. We'll turn our eyes toward the beauty of our Beloved. We'll find that the Spirit creates in us a new taste for that beauty, as well as eyes to see it in places as obvious as God's nature and Christ's love, and in the unexpected places of trials and temptations.

In part 2, we'll see how the Beloved we behold moves our hearts and *inclines* and *satisfies* the devoted mind. We'll discover that through our contemplation, the Spirit not only creates a new disposition of the mind but inclines our hearts toward God in the undivided love he calls us to and deserves. We'll reflect on the promised flourishing of the devoted mind in life and peace and deepen our grasp of what it means to find our rest in Christ alone (Matt. 11:29).

Reflection and Praxis

1. The subject of this book is "spiritual mindedness." What ideas do you already have about spiritual mindedness? What do you think Paul means by the phrase in Romans 8:6?

2. Do you know anyone you would describe as spiritually minded? What about them makes you think so?

3. Do you think of yourself as spiritually minded? Why do you think so? Describe the ways you are (or are not) spiritually minded.

4. What would you like God to do in your life as you read and reflect on this book? Write a brief prayer that seeks from him the grace for just that.

Here is mine: *Dear God my Father, as I write, prevent me from settling for secondhand spirituality. Grant me the grace to draw near to you in Christ and the grace to know your presence with me; help me to taste and see your goodness, to be satisfied with your beauty, and to love you with all my heart, all my soul, and all my mind. Amen.*

Part 1

contemplation

1

the devoted mind
is of the Spirit

For with You is the fountain of life.
—Psalm 36:9

The Doctrine of Provenance

Suppose you come into a little money and decide to acquire a Navajo rug. Not just any rug, but a historic treasure you'll not only admire and enjoy now but later pass to your daughter when you leave this old world. You set your eyes on a Two Grey Hills design from the 1920s. Before you drop your twelve grand, what should you do?

Verify the rug's provenance. You'll need to see a certificate of authenticity, something that confirms it is in fact a Two Grey Hills rug woven in the 1920s. You don't want your daughter to hear from an appraiser, "You've inherited a beautiful rug, and the *style* is Navajo, but it was woven in Mexico in the 2020s." The *sine qua non* of a Navajo rug and the measure of its value isn't only its artistry or its artisanship but its origin.

Spiritual mindedness, according to Paul, is a treasure. He appraises its value at "life and peace" (Rom. 8:6), and in our final chapter we'll see that "life and peace" is shorthand for our inheritance in Christ. If we think of spiritual mindedness as a fine rug, the fibers woven to create it are spiritual thoughts and longings. And the fundamental criterion by which the Great Appraiser will judge a mind—whether it is truly spiritual—is the origin, the fountain, of those thoughts. The *sine qua non* of a spiritual thought isn't its doctrinal precision or even its object but its origin.

The fountain of truly spiritual thoughts is the Holy Spirit.

That should sound familiar. In the introduction, I said that spiritual mindedness begins with the Holy Spirit. I'm repeating myself, but I need to elaborate on an implication of that truth.

In the next several chapters, we'll survey the objects of a spiritual mind. We'll consider what it thinks about, such as God's being and character, Christ's person and work, heaven, and things above. We'll look closely at each because we want to grow in spiritual mindedness. And because such thoughts are heady and even sublime, we can easily mistake deeper understanding of the doctrines of God, Christ, and heaven for growth in spiritual mindedness. It's true that deeper understanding is necessary for growth in spiritual mindedness, but it's not sufficient. A thought about God or Christ or heaven isn't spiritual just because it's about God or Christ or heaven; Satan trembles with thoughts of God and Christ, but his thoughts are demonic (James 2:19). Our thoughts must be born of the Spirit.

Growth by the Spirit

The Spirit sanctifies us throughout our lives. He matures us in holiness through a two-beat rhythm, enabling us more and more to put sin to death and to put on Christ (Rom. 8:13;

13:14). His sanctifying work extends through the farthest reaches of our hearts—our minds, wills, affections, and consciences—but our attention now is on the Spirit's sanctifying work on our minds.

As we put on Christ, our minds are "renewed in knowledge according to the image of Him who created [us]" (Col. 3:10). As our minds are renewed and we're being transformed, Paul warns each of us "not to think of himself more highly than he ought to think, but to think soberly, as God has dealt to each one a measure of faith" (Rom. 12:3). He says it's possible for us to misread our own maturity level. In other words, we might not yet be as spiritually minded as we think.

The art and skill to know ourselves well and weigh our spiritual mindedness isn't easy; it takes maturity. Over time we realize that as God prompts us to set our minds on things above—prompts us in his Word or in our prayers or in creation—even as believers we often respond to him "according to the flesh." Our thoughts of him can be abstract, barren notions. Yes, even as believers.

To know whether our thoughts are truly spiritual, we need to know whether they flow from the Spirit. Our gracious God provides a way we can test their provenance.

The Earmarks of the Spirit on Our Thoughts

When the appraiser examines your rug, he looks for the indicators that set Navajo rugs apart. He considers how faded the colors are, how worn the materials. He confirms that it's Churro wool, woven with a continuous warp thread. To verify that it's an original Two Grey Hills, he holds it up to the light to see the tight weave.

Similarly, the pattern and heft of our thoughts about spiritual things bear distinguishing earmarks of their origin. We hold

29

them up to the light of the Word and Spirit to inspect those marks. We look for the fruit of those thoughts in our love to others, the dead giveaway of the Spirit's work. When we see the earmarks of the Spirit, our confidence before God grows.

Spiritual Thoughts Come Freely

"If you had a month off and money were no object, where would you go?" An icebreaker like that reveals something about us. Whether we say we'd trek our way across Patagonia or dine our way across Paris, we reveal what we believe would refresh and recharge us. "When your mind has the evening off, where does it go?" That's a more revealing question because it's not hypothetical. Though work and family and domestic duties demand much of our attention, we all have discretionary time when our minds are free to roam.

And roam they do. But the Spirit renovates our minds. When we are born of the Spirit, he becomes in us "a fountain of water springing up into everlasting life" (John 4:14). The life he creates isn't everlasting just because it carries on without end. It is everlasting because it is life in communion with the eternal Father and Son by the Spirit (John 17:3). And the thoughts that bubble up freely in our minds savor of the Spirit, their source. Our minds begin to roam toward a new destination: our Beloved and all things in relation to our Beloved.

When your mind is free, whether you're walking in the forest primeval or on your treadmill in your garage, what fills it? When our minds are least constrained by the duties of the moment, we can best judge their inclination.

Spiritual Thoughts Proliferate

Remember, our sanctification is lifelong, and our thoughts and longings are at the center of that lifelong work. When we are born again in Christ and given his Spirit, we aren't instantly endowed with an undistractable interest in heavenly things. But our new minds, prompted by the new principle of life implanted in us, turn toward God. We turn to him in an arrow prayer[1] or in the words of a hymn, in mulling over memorized Scriptures or in puzzling out how best to live according to God's will in a sticky situation. We turn to him in set times of prayer and worship, in public and in private. We turn to him in sleepless hours at night and in the daily commuter traffic snarl. In the next two chapters, we'll see how we can turn to him in trials and temptations. And over the years, as the Spirit works and our minds and hearts are tuned more and more to God, we learn the blessedness of the one whose "delight is in the law of the LORD, and in His law he meditates day and night" (Ps. 1:2).

Spiritual Thoughts Delight

Another sign that the Spirit himself lies behind our thoughts of spiritual things is their effect on our hearts. When our minds are renewed, we pray not only because we're compelled by a sense of duty or because we need God to help us out of a mess. We pray because in prayer our hearts rest in the satisfying nearness of our Beloved. Paul tells us that through Christ we "have access by one Spirit to the Father" (Eph. 2:18). We meet our God in the holiest place, behind the veil (Heb. 10:19–20). In prayer we approach his throne of grace, and he welcomes us there (Heb. 4:16).

David describes this delight in God's presence—our faith's comprehensive taste of God's goodness, grace, mercy, and love:

---

1. A brief, welling-up-on-the-spot cry to God evoked by circumstances. It might be a cry of praise, contrition, or thanks or a cry for help for yourself or someone else.

31

How precious is Your lovingkindness, O God!
Therefore the children of men put their trust under the
    shadow of Your wings.
They are abundantly satisfied with the fullness of Your house,
And You give them drink from the river of Your pleasures.
For with You is the fountain of life;
In Your light we see light. (Ps. 36:7–9)

Spiritual Thoughts Transform

There is no smugness in the spiritual mind, no "God, I thank you that I am not like other men" (Luke 18:11). When the root of our thoughts is the Spirit, they produce his fruit: "Love, joy, peace, longsuffering, kindness, goodness, faithfulness, gentleness, self-control" (Gal. 5:22–23). And if the fruit of our thoughts is love, they do not puff us up in spiritual pride, for pride opposes love (1 Cor. 8:1). In fact, our thoughts are most certifiably spiritual when they humble us, while the flesh exalts itself in knowledge and the *appearance* of spiritual mindedness.

Thoughts that have their source in the Spirit aren't everything there is to life with God. As C. S. Lewis put it, "Thinking about worship is a different thing from worshipping."[2] And thinking about visiting "orphans and widows in their trouble" and keeping oneself "unspotted from the world" is different from visiting and keeping (James 1:27). If thoughts of God's holiness, no matter how precise and profound, don't provoke our own devotion to God and reverent worship of him and devoted service to him, they have no trace of the Spirit in them.

We might paraphrase James and say that spiritual thoughts without works are dead.

2. C. S. Lewis, *Letters to Malcolm: Chiefly on Prayer* (New York: Harcourt Brace Jovanovich, 1963, 1964), 4–5.

Search Me, O God

If spiritual thoughts flow and even overflow when the mind is free, and those overflowing thoughts delight and change us, then they are supernatural. They are earmarks of the Spirit's life in us. The way for us to see the Spirit's work in us, and to see where we need to grow, is by examining our hearts regularly.

Self-examination is a discipline. It's a duty we're called to, because without examining our hearts how could we admit that we are sinners and confess our sins (1 John 1:8–10)? To do it well, we need God's grace.[3] The way we examine ourselves—the way we obey all God's commands—is shaped by his grace. That might sound odd. But think about how Paul calls us to vigorous obedience: "Therefore, my beloved, as you have always obeyed . . . work out your own salvation with fear and trembling; for it is God who works in you both to will and to do for His good pleasure" (Phil. 2:12–13). God's gracious, empowering presence is the air our obedience breathes.

So what is God's grace in this discipline of self-examination? The freedom and light of the Spirit. The freedom of the Spirit is that our conviction of sin and failure is not condemnation but a call to turn to our Father in Christ (Rom. 8:1). The light of the Spirit illumines our hearts and minds: "O LORD, You have searched me and known me" (Ps. 139:1). David trusted God's Spirit to know him better than he knew himself, so he didn't search his own heart without help. He called on God:

Search me, O God, and know my heart;
Try me, and know my anxieties;
And see if there is any wicked way in me,
And lead me in the way everlasting. (Ps. 139:23–24)

3. Remember the phrase from Owen's title: *grace and duty*. Keep them together.

33

Self-examination, then, is done in faith and dependence, as we trust God to show us the truth about ourselves.

By the light of the Spirit, we see our hearts clearly. We lament how few thoughts we have of Christ and God and heaven and how brief and shallow those few thoughts are. We regret those wasteful times when we let our train of thought get dragged down another rabbit hole. And we mourn over and ask forgiveness for our negligence.

But the Spirit won't show us only our straying and wasted thoughts. It's God's fatherly disposition to be pleased with his children (Phil. 2:13). He sees all our secrets, including our holy thoughts, and rewards us (Matt. 6:4, 6). He trains and disciplines us so we will yield "the peaceable fruit of righteousness" (Heb. 12:11). He is "the God of patience and comfort" (Rom. 15:5). "He remembers that we are dust" (Ps. 103:14). So his Spirit not only convicts but confirms (Rom. 8:16; 1 John 3:24).

With this perspective, our self-examination itself becomes a time of communion with God, of renewal, of reconciliation, of drawing near to our Beloved.

This too is spiritual mindedness.

Reflection and Praxis

1. Regular prompts to spiritual mindedness include the acts of corporate worship: confessing sin, confessing faith, praying, singing, hearing the Scriptures read and preached, presenting tithes and offerings, celebrating the Lord's Supper, receiving God's benediction. Choose at least two or three acts from this list and write down ways these can become missed opportunities. (Obvious examples include daydreaming through the service or gathering your things to leave during the benediction. A less obvious example might be nursing a critical attitude toward the

selection of hymns.[4]) The goal of this exercise is to tune in to ways we squander prime times to fix our minds on things above.

2. Choose at least two or three acts of worship from the above list and write down ways you can turn them to your mind's spiritual advantage. (For example, if your church makes the order of worship available early, prepare the evening before by thinking through the content of the hymns so you will be able to sing them with understanding and delight.) The goal of this exercise is to tune in to ways we can train ourselves in the love-work of the mind.

3. Write a prayer in which you seek the help of the Spirit to examine your thought life in light of Colossians 3:1–3.

4. Assuming you have a stable schedule, review your regular routine to identify the times each day when your mind has no demands from family or work. Choose a time that you can most likely protect from distractions. Choose a discipline of spiritual mindedness, such as memorization and meditation on Scripture, prayer, or devotional reading that would fit that time. Commit the next seven days to that discipline. Consider using a journal to help you to connect your thoughts from day to day. After seven days, assess what you have done and determine whether to continue or try something else.

---

4. Music is a gift from God to deepen both our thoughts and longings toward him, but because people have strong opinions about it, we easily deform the gift into a stumbling block. For a clearheaded discussion of this from a concerned layman, see C. S. Lewis, "On Church Music," in *Christian Reflections*, ed. Walter Hooper (Grand Rapids: William B. Eerdmans, 1967 and 1995), 94–99.

2

the devoted mind seeks
the Beloved in hard places

My heart did heave, and there came forth, O God!
By that I knew that thou wast in the grief,
To guide and govern it to my relief,
Making a scepter of the rod:
Hadst thou not had thy part,
Sure the unruly sigh had broke my heart.
—GEORGE HERBERT

Where Can We Meet with God?

Seek God's face always. That is this book's theme, the essence
of spiritual mindedness, and it comes from Psalm 105:4. I've been
preaching it to myself lately, in one form or another, trying to
reform not just my thinking but the way I relate to my Beloved.
I know spiritual mindedness isn't limited to private devotions and
public worship. I know the devoted mind doesn't clock in and
clock out but presses on, not satisfied till Christ fills every corner
of life and meets us everywhere. But is it reasonable to think that
we can know God's presence everywhere, in any circumstance?

Can we know his presence during suffering and temptation? Or must we at times resign ourselves to enduring his absence?

The psalmists are preoccupied with seeking God's presence.[1] Of course, in every prayer we seek God: we seek him as Provider, Protector, Healer, and Savior. But often the psalmists long for pure communion with God, simply to be with him and to enjoy him—to seek him as their Beloved. So their prayers are a starting point for us to think about and stir up our own seeking.

If we turn first to Psalm 139, our expectations soar, for we find that God is not only accessible, but inescapable:

> Where can I go from Your Spirit?
> Or where can I flee from Your presence?
> If I ascend into heaven, You are there;
> If I make my bed in hell, behold, You are there.
> If I take the wings of the morning,
> And dwell in the uttermost parts of the sea,
> Even there Your hand shall lead me,
> And Your right hand shall hold me. (Ps. 139:7–10)

God's presence, it seems, is inevitable. And if Psalm 139 was all the psalmists said about our experience of God's presence, we would expect spiritual mindedness and communion with our Beloved to be as much a part of life as breathing. But of course there is more to the story.

The same David who confesses the inescapable God in Psalm 139 feels far from him in Psalm 42:

> My soul thirsts for God, for the living God.
> When can I go and meet with God? (Ps. 42:2 NIV)

---

1. See, for example, Psalms 9:10; 22:26; 24:6; 27:4, 8; 34:10; 40:16; 63:1; 69:32; 70:4; 105:3–4; and 119:2.

His sense of God's certain presence has vanished. And another psalmist, "the afflicted one" who prays Psalm 102, fears that God might willingly obscure his presence, even at the very point of his need:

> Do not hide Your face from me in the day of my trouble.
> (Ps. 102:2)

God hide his face from us? When we need him most? That, the worst of fears, is realized by the one who laments his loss of God's presence and comfort in Psalm 88:

> LORD, why do You cast off my soul?
> Why do You hide Your face from me? (Ps. 88:14)

And we bow in silence before the words of dereliction that Jesus cried out with a loud voice from the cross:

> My God, My God, why have You forsaken Me? (Ps. 22:1;
> see Matt. 27:46)

When we digest the implications of these prayers together, they teach us that the *fact* of God's presence is constant, but our *experience* of it can ebb and flow—to our frustration and even agony. The premise, then, of this and the next several chapters is that we can (and should) seek God's face everywhere, at any time, in any circumstance. Psalm 139 is the ground of our search and high hopes. Psalms 42, 102, and 88, however, remind us that we aren't yet in heaven and our experience of God's presence isn't unbroken; sometimes we will feel shut out, bereft of God.

But even that sense of God's absence isn't without purpose.

Nothing That Happens Is Happenstance

When Ruth and Naomi return to Bethlehem from Moab, they are widowed and impoverished. Naomi is bitter, because she feels that God has treated her bitterly and afflicted her (Ruth 1:20–21). Looking for relief from their poverty, Ruth goes into the fields to follow the reapers and pick up what they've left over—a means of provision for the poor in Israel (Ruth 2:2; see Lev. 19:9–10). The narrator tells us with a wink that Ruth "happened to come to the part of the field belonging to Boaz, who was of the family of Elimelech" (Ruth 2:3). "She happened to" can be more literally translated "her chance chanced upon"—an ironic reference to God's work through their circumstances. Boaz turns out to be their kinsman-redeemer, the one who is able to deliver them from their deprivation and disgrace. And though this "lucky break" shows God's individual care for Naomi and Ruth, he's also at work in it to redeem us all: Ruth and Boaz are David's great grandparents, ancestors of David's Greater Son to come.

By faith we know and confess that God is at work in everything that happens. Nothing that happens is happenstance. God's purposeful reign is comprehensive: he governs all his creatures and all their actions for his own ends.[2] And since he is infinitely wise (Ps. 147:5; Rom. 16:27), his providence can't be second-guessed, as if we, his creatures, knew better how to manage the universe (or even our own lives). Paul, no novice in the school of suffering, tells us that we who are God's children know that through our every sigh and groan he has in mind our

---

2. For brief definitions of providence, see the *Westminster Confession of Faith*, Chapter 5 and *The Belgic Confession*, Article 13. John Calvin is also concise and yet thorough in his *Institutes of the Christian Religion*, ed. John T. McNeill (Philadelphia: Westminster, 1960), 1.16.1–1.17.14 (hereafter cited as *Institutes*).

good, and the good he has in mind is that we become more and more like his Son (Rom. 8:18–29).

Given that space and time are saturated with God's active purpose, we know that our Beloved lives and works not only in the pages of his Word and in the bread and wine, but in what we call his *hard providence*: lost jobs, diseases that leave scars, accidents that take an eye or a limb, "precious friends hid in death's dateless night."[3] God even uses attention-grabbing providence not only to shape us but to draw us close.

In Hard Places, the Devoted Mind Seeks God as Father

Hard providence threatens to crush us, but because God knows how fragile we are, he teaches us to grieve. He does so especially through the fifty psalms of lament.[4] The devoted mind learns how to weep in the presence of God, how to commune with him as "the God of all comfort" (2 Cor. 1:3–5) or, sometimes, as the God who hides his face (Ps. 88:14).

I don't mean to make this sound simple, as if you could read a book or take a class to learn how to seek God through the hard places of life. Nothing about this is easy. But because God is Lord, because he is wise, because he is our Father, because he invites us to call on him "in the day of trouble" (Ps. 50:15), seeking his face along the roughest roads we walk is possible. I think it's even fair to say, looking to the example of the psalmists, that crying

3. William Shakespeare, sonnet 30. This is not to deny the unique place of the Word of God, the sacraments, and prayer as means of grace. In fact, they interpret and give meaning to our suffering. See the Westminster Shorter Catechism, question and answer 88.

4. For help learning from the psalms how to lament, see Richard L. Pratt, Jr., *Pray with Your Eyes Open* (Phillipsburg, NJ: Presbyterian and Reformed, 1987), 67–90.

out for deliverance is another way the devoted mind communes with God as Father (1 Peter 5:7), and it is perhaps a way we share in the fellowship of Christ's sufferings or at least imitate him (Phil. 3:10; compare Luke 22:41–44).

And the devoted mind, as it matures, knows that there can be more to our hardship, another layer, another path for us to seek and know God as Father and Lord. It's hard to see in the moment, but as we take time to reflect on our hardship, we can move closer to God. An example of this comes in Psalm 119, where we see the heightened sensitivity of the devoted mind.[5] Through 176 verses, the writer bares his heart. He's immersed in God's ways and almost bursts with delight in them. And in verse 67 he says that he cherishes God's discipline—the hard part of life—because it brings him back to God's path: "Before I was afflicted I went astray, but now I keep Your word." Looking back on his affliction, he sees God's presence in it and rejoices.

This isn't to dismiss our suffering, as if our great losses in life are just bad-tasting medicine we need to choke down for our own good. The point is that as we better and better know God as our wise Lord and Father, we will be able to move toward him and seek him even when we strain into a headwind, even in the dark.

To grow in spiritual mindedness, then, we can't listen to anyone who tells us that a hurricane or a heart attack is rotten luck or the hand of fate. If Christ is Lord of all, he is Lord of all our days and ways, and we bow before him. And if our Lord is holy, we know he hates sin and that, in his love for us sinners, he sometimes shakes our world till we see our sin.

We need to be careful here. The word *sometimes* means neither "always" nor "never." We can't *always* draw a line from a

---

5. Owen calls the psalmist's "constant delight in . . . the law of God" a pattern or model of spiritual mindedness; *The Works of John Owen*, 7:301.

particular hardship to a particular sin. That's the mistake of Job's friends, for which God rebukes them: they assume that by his sin he brought his trouble on his own head (Job 4:7–8; 5:17).

The disciples apparently didn't learn from Job's friends, for when they see a man born blind, they ask Jesus, "Rabbi, who sinned, this man or his parents, that he was born blind?" Jesus refuses their false dilemma: "Neither this man nor his parents sinned, but that the works of God should be revealed in him" (John 9:2–3).

Still, *sometimes* doesn't mean "never." At times God wields his rod of fatherly correction in love, so we stay alert, as Micah urged Israel: "Heed the rod and the One who appointed it" (Mic. 6:9 NIV). Hard providence is a call for us to examine ourselves and, depending on how the Spirit searches our hearts and what he reveals (Ps. 139:23–24), a call to honor God as Lord and Father and learn from his loving correction.

The writer of Hebrews even says discipline is a sign to us that God has adopted us, a sign of his love and care for us:

And you have forgotten the exhortation which speaks to you as to sons:

> "My son, do not despise the chastening of the LORD,
> Nor be discouraged when you are rebuked by Him;
> For whom the LORD loves He chastens,
> And scourges every son whom He receives."

If you endure chastening, God deals with you as with sons; for what son is there whom a father does not chasten? But if you are without chastening, of which all have become partakers, then you are illegitimate and not sons. Furthermore, we have had human fathers who corrected us, and we paid them respect. Shall we not much more readily be in subjection to the Father of spirits and live? For they indeed for a few days chastened us as seemed best to them, but He for our profit, that we may be partakers of His holiness. Now no chastening seems to be joyful for the present, but painful; nevertheless, afterward it yields the peaceable fruit of righteousness to those who have been trained by it. (Heb. 12:5–11)

The Son of God didn't suffer for his own sin but for ours. And "yet He learned obedience by the things which he suffered" (Heb. 5:8). Since God intends us "to be conformed to the image of His Son" (Rom. 8:29), we imitate the Son when we learn obedience from what we suffer; we grow in holiness. And note well the promise to those who grow in holiness: *they will see the Lord* (Heb. 12:14; see also Matt. 5:8).

To see the Beloved—that is the joy set before us, the joy of the devoted mind. For the hope of that joy, when we meet hard providence, we look for God in it, both in his comfort and his correction. We examine our consciences, and if we find some sin has ensnared us, we lay it aside. We do so to imitate Christ now and in the hope to see him later.

In Hard Places the Devoted Mind Is Weaned from the World

The devoted mind finds yet another good in the hard places, a good that the would-be disciple who comes to Jesus in Mark 10 needs. Jesus's words to the seeker sober us: "One thing you lack" (v. 21). Here is a man who not only knows God's commandments but has spent his life carefully keeping them. He may even recognize that Jesus is the Messiah; at least he knows that he is the Good Teacher who can tell him the way to eternal life. So far, so good. Yet Jesus says, "One thing you lack," and exposes that one thing with a diagnostic stress test: "Go your way, sell whatever you have and give to the poor, and you will have treasure in heaven; and come, take up the cross, and follow Me" (v. 21). But the would-be disciple "was sad at this word, and went away sorrowful, for he had great possessions" (v. 22).

The devoted mind refuses to lack even one thing. We want to rejoice in God's will on earth as it is in heaven (Matt. 6:10), to be satisfied with daily bread (Matt. 6:11), to seek first the kingdom of God and let him provide everything needed (Matt. 6:33), and to mature to the point that, in the face of the hardest providence, we can pray with Jesus in the garden, "Nevertheless, not as I will, but as You will" (Matt. 26:39).

Therefore we hear in hard providence God's appraisal of this world. Wildfires and flash floods remind us that houses, and all the things we spend our lives filling them with, fade faster than flowers. Cancer and arthritis remind us that "bodily exercise profits a little" (1 Tim. 4:8)—but only a little, because we're made of dust and to dust we will soon return (Gen. 3:19).

Our culture, deaf to God's way of reckoning, measures us by our ability to accumulate: more learning, more savvy, more power, more money, more gadgets. And because we believe that God's creation is good and that all we have is from him, we can be tempted to baptize the culture of accumulation in the name of God's bounty and goodness. The devoted mind recognizes this risk. We should, of course, receive all the good things God gives us with gratitude. But we must hold it all with Job's open hand, mindful that the Lord gives and the Lord takes away, and either way his name is blessed (Job 1:21).

If the loss of wealth or prestige or position in this world devastates us, can we honestly say we're content with God's will? If we sincerely desire to be devoted to God with all our minds, we'll let God's providence teach us the uncertainty and instability of earthly pleasures. We'll press even further, till we can "count it all joy when [we] fall into various trials, knowing that the testing of [our] faith produces patience" (James 1:2–3).

The only thing that can give us peace is to be free of dependence on the things of this life because we find real life in God alone. It is the one thing we need when Jesus puts us through the paces of his diagnostic stress test.

The Best Is Yet to Come

At the beginning of this chapter, I said the devoted mind cannot rest till Christ fills every corner of life. That straining effort to commune with the Beloved even in the face of pain, loss, and (in the next chapter) temptation marks the devotion of the devoted mind. This chapter was hard, and the next will be dark. But press on: we'll make our way to thoughts of heaven, of God, of Christ. We will seek the Beloved everywhere. And he will meet us where we seek him.

Reflection and Praxis

1. This is not an easy exercise: Recall a rough or even an unbearable time you've had to endure. Think about how you related to God through it. Did you draw closer to him? Were you able to express your grief and fear to him? Did you seek his help? Did your conscience alert you to any sin the Lord might be calling you to turn from? Did you perhaps leave God at a distance? Or did you even harden your heart in bitterness to God? What are some ways you might have related to God that would have matured you through the trial? If you think of any, make some notes about them. Then pray to God in gratitude or repentance or whatever else might help you to grow from the trial and draw closer to him now.

2. God teaches us in his Word how to lament hard things in life. He also teaches us to call on him in the day of trouble. And he teaches us to be content with his will. Is there a way to do all that simultaneously? Explain.

Suggestion for Further Reading

This short chapter is only a starting point and can't address many of the hard questions about suffering and how to stay close to God through it. Timothy Keller, in his *Walking with God through Pain and Suffering* (New York: Dutton, 2013), provides a warm, fuller guide to understanding the place of suffering in the Christian life, as well as how to stay close to our Beloved through suffering.

3

the devoted mind seeks
the Beloved in dark places

By the mystery of thy holy Incarnation; by thy holy Nativity and Circumcision; by thy Baptism, Fasting, and Temptation,
Good Lord, deliver us.

By thine Agony and bloody Sweat; by thy Cross and Passion; by thy precious Death and Burial; by thy glorious Resurrection, and Ascension; and by the coming of the Holy Ghost,
Good Lord, deliver us.
—THE LITANY (BOOK OF COMMON PRAYER 1662)

Difficulty and Danger, Risk and Readiness

When we understand how difficult and dangerous something will be, we know what's at stake and can better prepare for it. The Saffir-Simpson Hurricane Wind Scale, for example, warns coastal dwellers that an approaching category 1 storm could take shingles off roofs and break branches from trees, and a category 5 storm promises catastrophic damage. The Yosemite Decimal System alerts mountain climbers to the difficulty of their terrain:

class 1 is hiking on level ground, class 3 requires scrambling with hands and perhaps a rope; at class 4 "a fall could be fatal," and at class 5 "rock climbing begins in earnest."[1] The Defense Readiness Condition is also a five-tiered scale, but the severity levels work in the opposite direction: DEFCON 5 indicates peacetime conditions, and at DEFCON 1 we are at war.

If there were a similar five-tiered scale to rate the difficulty of being spiritually minded in various conditions, class 1 might include corporate worship and private prayer, which require rudimentary self-discipline. On such a scale, class 5 would surely include the challenge of seeking God's face *while being tempted to sin*. This is where spiritual mindedness begins in earnest.

Head-to-Head Combat

I include temptation in class 5 of my hypothetical scale because temptation fights for the same space in our hearts and minds that should be set on the Spirit. Whether the enemy is Satan or the world or the remnants of our unmortified flesh, the recipe is the same: Divert the mind and fix its thoughts on retribution or domination or preferment or superiority or gratification or bigger barns to store our bigger things (Luke 12:18). Stew those thoughts long enough and they harden into sinful acts and risk catastrophic damage to ourselves and others.

Temptation is most destructive when it provokes a batch of thoughts about sin and the expected pleasure it promises. For example, when as a young man I felt I had been wrongfully dismissed from my job, I lay awake many nights nursing my grievance and plotting revenge. I fixed on the dark idea of finding my boss's address, getting a sharp knife, and slashing

---

1. *Mountaineering: The Freedom of the Hills*, ed. Ronald C. Eng, 8th ed. (Seattle: Mountaineers Books, 2010), 564.

his tires. I almost convinced myself that if I could cause him some loss and frustration, I would balance the scales of justice and taste satisfaction.

When temptation captures our thoughts like this and we stay fixed on the sin itself and especially the pleasure it promises, we're in trouble. We will, if we have the means and opportunity, carry through with what we contemplate. The prophet Micah says as much, in a passage disturbingly reminiscent of my vandalistic fantasies:

> Woe to those who devise iniquity,
> And work out evil on their beds!
> At morning light they practice it,
> Because it is in the power of their hand. (Mic. 2:1)

Recall the principle that underlies this book: contemplation of our Beloved (mind-work) leads to inclination toward and satisfaction in him (heart-work). Our enemy understands how we are made and therefore tempts us to set our minds instead on worldly things. He knows that if our minds are captured, our hearts will follow. As Paul said in our key verse, "To set the mind on the flesh is death" (Rom. 8:6 ESV). James traces this chain from desire and contemplation to sin (and on to death):

> But each one is tempted when he is drawn away by his own desires and enticed. Then, when desire has conceived, it gives birth to sin; and sin, when it is full-grown, brings forth death. (James 1:14–15)

This is the path we'll follow unless we exercise faith in Christ Jesus and the sufficiency of his grace for our deliverance. The key to class 5 spiritual mindedness, to seeking God's face when we are tempted, is this: to think on the love, care, compassion, and tenderness of Christ—his ability to help, relieve, and save us from Satan. As we exercise faith in Christ Jesus, it strengthens us against temptation. Exercising our faith is the work of the Spirit in us.

The Way of Escape

Read these three texts together:

Therefore, in all things He had to be made like His brethren, that He might be a merciful and faithful High Priest in things pertaining to God, to make propitiation for the sins of the people. For in that He Himself has suffered, being tempted, He is able to aid those who are tempted. (Heb. 2:17–18)

For we do not have a High Priest who cannot sympathize with our weaknesses, but was in all points tempted as we are, yet without sin. Let us therefore come boldly to the throne of grace, that we may obtain mercy and find grace to help in time of need. (Heb. 4:15–16)

No temptation has overtaken you except such as is common to man; but God is faithful, who will not allow you to be tempted beyond what you are able, but with the temptation will also make the way of escape, that you may be able to bear it. (1 Cor. 10:13)

Now carefully consider what these verses affirm about Christ's love and care for us in the face of temptation.

Who are these texts talking about? Hebrews 2:18 identifies the objects of our High Priest's mercy as "those who are tempted." The one who helps, of course, is Christ, our "merciful and faithful High Priest" (Heb. 2:17).

What help does Christ give to those who are being tempted? Christ gives mercy and grace. His mercy is that he forgives us where we need to be forgiven, and he provides a way to escape temptation, which is his grace.

When does Christ help those who are being tempted? According to Hebrews 4:16, Christ helps us by his mercy and grace exactly when we are being tempted.

Where do we find his help? According to Hebrews 4:16, Christ helps us at the throne of grace.

Why does he help? It might sound strange to ask *why*, but this is where the love-work of the devoted mind begins in earnest. Let's slow down and take this in point by point.

- Christ helps us because he was "made like his brethren" (Heb. 2:17), a phrase which refers to his incarnation and mission.
- He freely and gladly accepted his mission from the Father (John 10:17–18).
- His mission was to "be a merciful and faithful High Priest in things pertaining to God, to make propitiation for the sins of the people" (Heb. 2:17).
- Further, "He Himself has suffered, being tempted" (Heb. 2:18), which enables him to help us when we are tempted.
- His being tempted also moves his human heart to sympathy for "our weaknesses" and makes him ready to welcome us to his "throne of grace" (Heb. 4:15–16).
- Note especially the title for his throne: it's a throne where the King lavishes grace on his beloved.

In other words, the short answer to the question "Why does he help?" is *love*.

How does he help? Hebrews 4:16 says, "Therefore come boldly to the throne of grace." That is, we approach him with our pleas for help, our prayers. And the *therefore* reminds us what motivates and even compels us to come: the nature and character of our High Priest. He embraced the mission to share our humble nature so he could suffer for us and be subjected to temptation like us. His love for us charms our fears and makes his throne a safe place to approach and a safe place to settle.

Even if all that is clear, we still have to learn how to exercise our faith in Christ in the face of temptation. That's a lifelong project. We should get started.

Poems, Prayers, and Practice Swings

Christina Rossetti understood that her Beloved on his throne of grace was her way of escape. In the following dialogue, Satan dangles before her heart the world's pleasure, glory, knowledge, and power. Her responses to him show how a soul turns to and leans on Christ on the front lines of temptation. Listen and note that at each point she rebuffs the devil not by her own force of will but by an appeal to Christ's character and life, his redemptive acts on her behalf—his love for her. When provoked by temptation, she communes with Christ. Satan speaks first:

"Thou drinkest deep."
"When Christ would sup
He drained the dregs from out my cup:
So how should I be lifted up?"

"Thou shalt win Glory."
"In the skies,
Lord Jesus, cover up mine eyes
Lest they should look on vanities."

"Thou shalt have Knowledge."
    "Helpless dust!
In Thee, O Lord, I put my trust:
Answer Thou for me, Wise and Just."

"And Might."—
    "Get thee behind me. Lord,
Who hast redeemed and not abhorred
My soul, oh keep it by Thy Word."[2]

On paper these simple verses make the way of escape look easy. But in real time, when fantasies about worldly glory and power and pleasure invade your mind in vibrant color, you are in class 5, where spiritual mindedness begins in earnest. When a boss humiliates you in front of your colleagues and you are overwhelmed by shame, anger will flood your heart faster than your mind can turn to the throne of grace. But this doesn't mean that exercising the devoted mind's faith is a futile endeavor. Rossetti's simple dialogue is a pattern that can train our minds and hearts through our lifelong project. Baseball helps us to understand how.

As a boy I played baseball, and I still remember the mind-numbing repetitiveness of practice. The coach hit "numberless infinities" of grounders to the short stop. Grounders right at him. Then to his left. Then to his right. Over and over, training that muscle memory, till the short stop could field a grounder backhanded, pivot, and throw to first base without thinking.

Once the players have their instincts burned in, they apply them in a game, when it isn't the coach hitting grounders but an opponent who might hit the ball anywhere. Then there's the pitch, the swing, the ball in play—and all those rehearsed

2. Christina Rossetti, from "The Three Enemies," in *Poems and Prose*, ed. Jan Marsh (London: Everyman, 1994), 25–26.

reactions kick in, and in half a second a dozen things happen. It was all prepared for and executed according to the basics of baseball, rehearsed ad infinitum. When it's done well, everyone tastes the thrill of beautiful play.

Similarly, we can train our hearts for those heated moments of temptation, developing over years of grace-filled self-discipline a kind of spiritual muscle memory. It can become the habit of our hearts, when we're ambushed by the world, the flesh, or the devil, to pivot and fire an arrow prayer to the throne of grace—to turn toward our Beloved and his loving protection.

This takes maturity gained through a life of walking with Christ. We fall, rise, and walk again.

Reflection and Praxis

1. Think about a recent time when you resisted temptation—when God by his grace provided the way of escape. What means did God use? Did he bring some Scripture to mind? Did the Spirit give you a sense of God's love that made you not want to sin against him (Gen. 39:8–9)? Is there some lesson in this for your own growth in spiritual mindedness? How might you seek God's face in the face of temptation?

2. This is an exercise to train your heart to respond to temptation by turning to the throne of grace the way Christina Rossetti does in the poem quoted above.

Step 1. Write down some of the temptations that often overwhelm you.

Step 2. Write a brief temptation-and-response dialogue, following either the model in the poem by Rossetti or the greater model she followed in the temptation of our Lord

(Matt. 4:1–11; Luke 4:1–13). In your dialogue, base the tempter's words on a specific temptation you noted in step 1. Base your response to the tempter on the character and work of Christ, his love for you, and your appeal to him. Below are some examples.

TEMPTER: You've been wronged!
MY SOUL: Wasn't my Lord wronged, yet he answered not one word (Matt. 27:14; 1 Peter 2:23)? And hasn't he promised that vengeance on my behalf belongs to him (Rom. 12:19–21)? Lord, grant me restraint and love!

TEMPTER: Look into those eyes: he (or she) desires you.
MY SOUL: My Lord had no beauty that he should be desired—we hid our faces from him and despised him (Isa. 53:2–3), and he was despised so that God might desire me. He is preparing a place for me and wants me to be with him where he is (John 14:2–3). Lord, may your desire and only your desire overpower me!

TEMPTER: You are alone: no one will see.
MY SOUL: Christ taught me that my Father sees me in secret and honors my faithfulness (Matt. 6:4). Lord, teach my faith to always trust that you see me and that you see me with the Father's eyes.

3. For those who memorize Scripture for meditation (and for those who want to start), memorize the passages we studied in "The Way of Escape." Commit them to heart so that you can recite them as if they were your words. Then review them weekly to keep them close to the surface of your heart. When temptation comes, flee to the throne of grace. Appeal to the promises in these verses as you seek from Christ a way of escape.

Suggestions for Further Reading

John Owen's three main treatises on temptation and our struggle with the flesh are the gold standard; Kelly M. Kapic and Justin Taylor have helpfully edited them in *Overcoming Sin and Temptation* (Wheaton, IL: Crossway Books, 2006); I have also adapted Owen's books on sin and temptation in *The Enemy Within: Straight Talk about the Power and Defeat of Sin* (Phillipsburg, NJ: P&R Publishing, 2023).

4

the devoted mind seeks the Beloved in high places

The heavens are calling you, and wheel around you,
Displaying to you their eternal beauties,
And still your eye is looking on the ground.
—DANTE

Running at Altitude

Some years ago—never mind how long precisely—in the days when I could say to my body "Run!" and my body would ask how far, I spent a week in the Sangre de Cristo Mountains of southern Colorado. I had been living and running in the desert of southern New Mexico, and our camp in Colorado, at nine thousand feet above sea level, was almost a mile higher than home.

When I hit the trail for my first morning run at altitude, the crisp summer mountain air refreshed and invigorated me—for about a hundred yards. Then it vanished into thin air. I slowed down to regulate my breathing. My heaving chest made me doubt my fitness. I wasn't ready for such heights.

Contemplating at Altitude

One reader of early drafts of this chapter shied at the idea of contemplating heaven. He said he felt afloat and frightened at the prospect. I was glad he said so, because he speaks for many. And it's no wonder: our minds aren't acclimated to such heights of thought. When Paul, who had trained his mind and heart at altitude,[1] contemplated the mysteries of God's wisdom and sovereignty, he found himself out of breath: "Oh, the depth of the riches both of the wisdom and knowledge of God! How unsearchable are His judgments and His ways past finding out!" (Rom. 11:33). The first words of verse 33 in the Latin Vulgate are "*O altitudo!*"

As strenuous and demanding as it is, Paul nevertheless tells us to fill our minds with thoughts of heaven just as we fill our lungs with mountain air:

> If then you were raised with Christ, seek those things which are above, where Christ is, sitting at the right hand of God. Set your mind on things above, not on things on the earth. (Col. 3:1–2)

Heaven is where Christ is seated at the right hand of God, and that's where our minds must be.

This isn't easy. As soon as we hit the trail, we'll find out what it means to be a finite creature in the presence of an eternally holy God. God's glory in heaven, infinite and incomprehensible, overwhelms us. Like a landslide.

If we survive the landslide of God's glory, we still have obstacles; until we're acclimated, we're short of *light* and *delight*. By

---

1. See 2 Corinthians 12:1–10, where Paul discloses, trying not to boast, that he was taken into the third heaven.

light, I mean know-how—we haven't yet learned how to think about heaven and heavenly things. By *delight*, I mean we haven't yet sampled the sweetness of thoughts of heaven, so we don't yet have a taste for them. I suspect many of us don't think much of heaven at all until we find ourselves close to the door. At that point, our thoughts of heaven are in-case-of-emergency-break-glass thoughts. But since such thoughts haven't been our daily bread, we may find them hard to swallow.

It's different for the devoted mind. If we often, even daily, set our minds on heaven, our minds will adjust to the altitude and the heavenly light. When I was running in Colorado, I gasped at first but pressed on. Each day my lungs felt less distress. The only day I didn't run, I climbed Horn Peak, pushing myself in high places. And that single week of training at altitude changed my body. I've never felt stronger than when I got home and did my first run in the valley. I shaved minutes off my personal best for three miles. Of course, after just a few days without those runs at altitude, my body settled back to its old normal.

Likewise, if we look up, up to heaven where Christ is, and fix our gaze, we'll not only learn how to think of heavenly things but find ourselves changed. Paul says that if we look at the things that are unseen, the eternal things, day by day we will be renewed, and God will work in us an eternal weight of glory:

> Therefore we do not lose heart. Even though our outward man is perishing, yet the inward man is being renewed day by day. For our light affliction, which is but for a moment, is working for us a far more exceeding and eternal weight of glory, while we do not look at the things which are seen, but at the things which are not seen. For the things which are seen are temporary, but the things which are not seen are eternal. (2 Cor. 4:16–18)

Grace upon Grace upon Grace upon Grace

Because he is Lord, God justly commands our obedience. But unlike other lords, he puts his law in our minds and writes it on our hearts (Jer. 31:33; Heb. 8:10; 10:16). He lives in us by his Spirit (1 Cor. 6:19). He works in us "both to will and to do for His good pleasure" (Phil. 2:13). Remember Owen's title, *The Grace and Duty of Being Spiritually Minded*. Our *duty*, which we take up with loving vigor, is saturated by his *grace*. Praise him!

What's more, our gracious Lord attaches to his commands some completely gratuitous incentives. In this case, when we obey his command and direct our eyes to heaven, we can expect God to bolster both our faith and our hope.

Fortified Faith

Hebrews 11:1 says that the objects of faith are "things not seen." So when we think of heaven and heavenly things, we exercise faith. Exercising faith fortifies and expands it, the way squats and push-ups build strength and endurance.

When we put our faith to work in fixing our thoughts on heaven, we grow more assured of the reality of heaven. In fact, if we don't often think of heavenly things, we won't as surely believe they exist. A feeble faith in the reality of heaven can undermine the whole course of our walk with God.

Think about how often in the Scriptures heaven is held before us to encourage our endurance through trials and persecution. If the reality of heaven isn't firmly fixed in our minds—not as a generic goodness but in its concrete glory—how can it stir us up to love and good works, make us ready to bear our crosses, or wean us from an inordinate love of the world?

But the Spirit enables us to search "the deep things of God," especially the unseen "things which God has prepared for those who love him" (1 Cor. 2:9–10).

High Hopes

We talk often of living by faith, since faith is how we come to know God through Jesus Christ. But what about hope? How often do we think of our life in terms of it? Yet hope is the fruit of faith in God, the expectation that he will keep all his promises to us, and the longing for that promised glory. Paul even makes hope sound like the capstone of the work of God's grace in us:

> Therefore, having been justified by faith, we have peace with God through our Lord Jesus Christ, through whom also we have access by faith into this grace in which we stand, and rejoice in hope of the glory of God. And not only that, but we also glory in tribulations, knowing that tribulation produces perseverance; and perseverance, character; and character, hope. Now hope does not disappoint, because the love of God has been poured out in our hearts by the Holy Spirit who was given to us. (Rom. 5:1–5)

Consider further how hope is portrayed in the New Testament:

- Our God is the God of hope. He makes us overflow with hope by faith in Christ, so that we have joy and peace (Rom. 15:13).
- Hope, along with faith and love, endures (1 Cor. 13:13).
- Hope looks forward with expectation to heaven (Col. 1:5).
- Hope enables our patience (1 Thess. 1:3).
- Hope is a gift of God's grace (2 Thess. 2:16).
- Our hope is to see "our great God and Savior Jesus Christ" (Titus 2:13).

- We hope in eternal life (Titus 3:7).
- By this hope we draw near to God behind the veil (Heb. 6:19; 7:19).
- Hope motivates our sanctification (1 John 3:3).
- And perhaps the highest expression of hope's greatness is that it is the work of Christ in us: "Christ in you, the hope of glory" (Col. 1:27).

Like faith, hope strengthens us along the way, lifts our hearts under hardship, deepens our joy in Christ, and keeps us close to him. And hope, like faith, is reinforced by frequent thoughts of heaven, where our hope lives (Col. 1:5).

Getting Started

Once we're convinced from the Scriptures that it's our duty to "set our minds on things above" (Col. 3:2), on "the things which are not seen" (2 Cor. 4:18), and when we're motivated by God's gracious assurances of the benefits of heavenly mindedness, we want to know how. And one thing we must always keep in mind is that our ideas of heaven must be biblical. Yes, our imaginations help our faith to see fuller and richer implications of what the Bible says about heaven, but we must start from what God tells us and anchor our thoughts in his Word.

Learning how to set our minds on things above is a lifelong project. We'll start with a few basic biblical truths to build on, then look at some examples of master builders.

Heaven Is Deliverance *From*

Heaven is the complete, final, and everlasting deliverance from every form of evil, harm, pain, torment, and trouble. Paul says that those believers who have been persecuted in this world will find rest from those who trouble them (2 Thess. 1:7). One of the elders before the throne of the Lamb in Revelation tells John that those who come through the

> great tribulation . . . shall neither hunger anymore nor thirst anymore; the sun shall not strike them, nor any heat; for the Lamb who is in the midst of the throne will shepherd them and lead them to living fountains of waters. And God will wipe away every tear from their eyes. (Rev. 7:14–17)

For believers, the greatest burden of this life is our own sin. The memory of it, the struggle with it, the frustration and shame of it make us cry, "O wretched man that I am! Who will deliver me from this body of death?" (Rom. 7:24). Although the gospel of forgiveness and the comfort of the Spirit ease the agony of those thoughts in this life, we look forward to the final lifting of that burden from our hearts and minds; in heaven there will be no more sin. Nothing sinful will be allowed through the gates (Rev. 21:27). We will be conformed to the image of Christ, our sanctification completed, and our nature glorified in him (1 John 3:2).

Heaven Is Deliverance *To*

Of course heaven is much more than relief from suffering. It is the Father's house, filled with mansions, where Christ is preparing a place for us—and he will come to take us there (John 14:2–3). He'll come for us because he wants us to be with him and to see his glory (John 17:24). There "the tabernacle of God is with men, and He will dwell with them, and they shall be His people. God Himself will be with them and be their God" (Rev. 21:3). In his presence we will have "fullness of joy," because "at [His] right hand are pleasures forevermore" (Ps. 16:11). Our nature will not only be purified in its cleansing from sin but also perfected and glorified so that we will have the capacity and ability to commune with God forever, "always conversing with God in new ways," as Irenaeus put it.[2] This is what John saw:

> And he showed me a pure river of water of life, clear as crystal, proceeding from the throne of God and of the Lamb. In the middle of its street, and on either side of the river, was the tree of life, which bore twelve fruits, each tree yielding its fruit every month. The leaves of the tree were for the healing of the nations. And there shall be no more curse, but the throne of God and of the Lamb shall be in it, and His servants shall serve Him. They shall see His face. (Rev. 22:1–4)

That's what we're made for.

Contemplating Heaven and Heavenly Things

What do we do with these basic biblical teachings about heaven? The art of setting our minds on things above begins with those truths. Meditating on them is an act of faith extended by imagination. Many believers are gifted at this, and we can learn from them. Two master contemplators of heaven are Jonathan Edwards and George Herbert.

As you read and pray through each of the examples below, try to see the connection from the biblical truth to the vision of heaven that is the fruit of contemplation. And note how it affects you, how it moves you.

Master Class with Jonathan Edwards

Jonathan Edwards is often remembered for his visceral rhetoric in a sermon on God's wrath,[3] but he could speak with equal force

2. Irenaeus, *Against Heresies*, 5.36.1.
3. Jonathan Edwards, "Sinners in the Hands of an Angry God."

of God's love. In his final sermon on 1 Corinthians 13, "Heaven a World of Charity or Love," Edwards models contemplation of heaven. His method is to trace biblical themes along their trajectory into eternity, so that by faith we contemplate that unseen world.

For example, Paul says that love does not envy and is not proud (1 Cor. 13:4). Edwards imagines what a world emptied of envy and pride would be like; he extrapolates those perfections of love to their fullness and treats us to a picture of undiluted love among the saints in heaven. (You might find Edwards easier to follow if you read this selection out loud.)

> And when there is perfect satisfaction, there can be no reason for envy. And there will be no temptation for any to envy those that are above them in glory, on account of the latter being lifted up with pride, for there will be no pride in heaven. . . . The saints that are highest in glory will be the lowest in humbleness of mind, for their superior humility is part of their superior holiness. . . .
>
> And besides, the inferior in glory will have no temptation to envy those that are higher than themselves, for those that are highest will not only be more loved by the lower for their higher holiness, but they will also have more of the spirit of love to others, and so will love those that are below them more than if their own capacity and elevation were less. They that are highest in degree in glory, will be of the highest capacity; and so having the greatest knowledge, will see most of God's loveliness, and consequently will have love to God and love to the saints most abounding in their hearts. And on this account those that are lower in glory will not envy those that are above them, because they will be most beloved by those that are highest in glory.[4]

4. Jonathan Edwards, *Charity and Its Fruits; or, Christian Love as Manifested*

In this second sample from the same sermon, Edwards turns our attention to the unveiled presence of the Triune God, the fountain of love and all our blessedness in heaven:

There dwells God the Father, who is the father of mercies, and so the father of love, who so loved the world as to give his only-begotten Son to die for it. There dwells Christ, the Lamb of God, the prince of peace and of love, who so loved the world that he shed his blood, and poured out his soul unto death for men. There dwells the great Mediator, through whom all the divine love is expressed toward men, and by whom the fruits of that love have been purchased, and through whom they are communicated, and through whom love is imparted to the hearts of all God's people. There dwells Christ in both his natures, the human and the divine, sitting on the same throne with the Father. And there dwells the Holy Spirit—the Spirit of divine love, in whom the very essence of God, as it were, flows out and is breathed forth in love, and by whose immediate influence all holy love is shed abroad in the hearts of all the saints on earth and in heaven. There, in heaven, this infinite fountain of love—this eternal Three in One—is set open without any obstacle to hinder access to it, as it flows for ever. There this glorious God is manifested, and shines forth, in full glory, in beams of love. And there this glorious fountain for ever flows forth in streams, yea, in rivers of love and delight, and these rivers swell, as it were, to an ocean of love, in which the souls of the ransomed may bathe with the sweetest enjoyment, and their hearts, as it were, be deluged with love![5]

---

in the Heart and Life, ed. Tryon Edwards (New York: Robert Carter & Brothers, 1854), 482–83.

5. Edwards, 469–70.

Master Class with George Herbert

I'll close this chapter with George Herbert's masterpiece, "Love (III)."[6] Like Edwards, he starts from a biblical promise and image of heaven—in this case from Jesus's blessing in Luke 12:37 on "those servants whom the master, when he comes, will find watching." Jesus says that "he will gird himself and have them sit down to eat, and will come and serve them." From Jesus's image, Herbert creates a scene at an inn. The Innkeeper (whose name is Love) meets the weary traveler at the door to welcome him. (There are no quotation marks, but carefully note the two voices in dialogue.)

> Love bade me welcome: yet my soul drew back,
> Guilty of dust and sin.
> But quick-ey'd Love, observing me grow slack
> From my first entrance in,
> Drew nearer to me, sweetly questioning,
> If I lack'd anything.
>
> A guest, I answer'd, worthy to be here:
> Love said, You shall be he.
> I the unkind, ungrateful? Ah my dear,
> I cannot look on thee.
> Love took my hand, and smiling did reply,
> Who made the eyes but I?
>
> Truth Lord, but I have marr'd them: let my shame
> Go where it doth deserve.
> And know you not, says Love, who bore the blame?
> My dear, then I will serve.

6. George Herbert, *The Complete Poetry*, eds. John Drury and Victoria Moul (United Kingdom: Penguin Books, 2015), 180–81.

You must sit down, says Love, and taste my meat:
So I did sit and eat.

O altitudo!

Reflection and Praxis

1. Have you ever faced a particular struggle, such as a severe illness or the loss of someone you loved, and found help and hope in thoughts of heaven? If so, describe how. What aspects of heaven gave you comfort? Were your thoughts more of God's presence in heaven, seeing Christ, worshipping or communing with other saints there, or what?

2. Choose a biblical passage about heaven, such as John 14:1–7, 2 Corinthians 5:1–8, or Revelation 7:9–17. For the next week, spend about five minutes each day meditating on the unseen realities the text suggests. To see how your thoughts develop over the week, write down a thought or two each day. At the end of the week, review your notes and write a prayer to God that expresses the longings stirred in you by your meditations.

Suggestion for Further Reading

Stephen R. Morefield, in his *Always Longing: Discovering the Joy of Heaven* (Austin, TX: GCD Books, 2022), whets our appetite for heaven; he especially addresses those reluctant to think about it.

5

the devoted mind seeks the glory of Christ

*Every day we may see some new thing in Christ. His love
hath neither brim nor bottom.*
—Samuel Rutherford

Beyond Belief

Which is hardest for you to believe: that the sun stood still
in the sky for a day, that a donkey told Balaam to stop beating
her, or that God became man? We would assume all three are
myths if they weren't in God's Word.[1] But there is one thing in
the Bible that I find even harder to believe.

On the night in which he was betrayed, our Lord Jesus told
his disciples,

> In My Father's house are many mansions; if it were not so,
> I would have told you. I go to prepare a place for you. And
> if I go and prepare a place for you, I will come again and

1. See Joshua 10:1–14, Numbers 22:22–30, and John 1:1–18.

receive you to Myself; that where I am, there you may be also. (John 14:2–3)

That where I am, there you may be also. The Lord of Glory wants us to be with him? Not likely. I think he knew how far-fetched that would sound, because he adds "if it were not so, I would have told you" (v. 2). Truth himself says to us, as it were, "Would I lie to you?" And later that night, he goes farther when he prays for all who would believe in him, "Father, I desire that they also whom You gave Me may be with Me where I am, that they may behold My glory which You have given Me" (John 17:24).

He's made his desire clear. Yet, knowing the weakness of our faith, Jesus goes even farther; he moves beyond assurance and reassurance and holy prayer to a demonstration. How could he show his desire to be with us? In Acts 7, as the Jews reach for stones to martyr Stephen for his witness to Christ, Jesus lets him (and us) see into heaven:

But [Stephen], being full of the Holy Spirit, gazed into heaven and saw the glory of God, and Jesus standing at the right hand of God, and said, "Look! I see the heavens opened and the Son of Man standing at the right hand of God!" (Acts 7:55–56)

Instead of his royal posture seated at God's right hand to rule, Jesus stands. He stands in anticipation, eager to receive and welcome his beloved.

Later, John tells us what we can expect when Jesus welcomes us: "Beloved, now we are children of God; and it has not yet been revealed what we shall be, but we know that when He is revealed, we shall be like Him, for we shall see Him as He is" (1 John 3:2). Our face-to-face sight of Christ, once the weakness of our corruptible flesh has been removed so that we can see his majesty and yet live, will change us; his glory will spread through us and glorify us. "We shall be like him."

Even with Jesus's repetition and reassurance of his desire for us, even though we hear him tell the Father that he desires us to be with him, even though he opens the window into heaven for us to see his readiness, even with the ineffable promise that we will see him and be changed by that vision into his likeness, I find this hard to believe.

What pushes this to the boundaries of my belief is the fairy-tale distance between our Great High King and us scullery maids. How is it that the Son of God takes an interest in us? After all,

> He is the image of the invisible God, the firstborn over all creation. For by Him all things were created that are in heaven and that are on earth, visible and invisible, whether thrones or dominions or principalities or powers. All things were created through Him and for Him. And He is before all things, and in Him all things consist. And He is the head of the body, the church, who is the beginning, the firstborn from the dead, that in all things He may have the preeminence. (Col. 1:15–18)

Christ is exalted far above the unseen rulers of the heavenly realms. And we, though made "a little lower than the angels" (Ps. 8:5), have by our sin made ourselves pariahs and "children of wrath" (Eph. 2:3). In Ezekiel 16, God describes Israel as he found her; the image makes us turn away.

> As for your nativity, on the day you were born your navel cord was not cut, nor were you washed in water to cleanse you; you were not rubbed with salt nor wrapped in swaddling cloths. No eye pitied you, to do any of these things for you, to have compassion on you; but you were thrown out into

the open field, when you yourself were loathed on the day
you were born.

And when I passed by you and saw you struggling in
your own blood, I said to you in your blood, "Live!" Yes,
I said to you in your blood, "Live!" I made you thrive like a
plant in the field; and you grew, matured, and became very
beautiful. Your breasts were formed, your hair grew, but you
were naked and bare. (Ezek. 16:4–7)

We have no reason to think that we were any more desirable
than Israel when God found us, yet he reached down, all the way
down; he took us under his wing and made us his bride. Therefore
with Ruth we bow our faces to the ground and say, "Why have
I found favor in your eyes, that you should take notice of me?"
(Ruth 2:10). Why indeed? But it is the Father's pleasure to give
the Son what he asks.

He asks for us.

Paul tells us that the best of all things comes at the end of all
things, when "we shall always be with the Lord" (1 Thess. 4:17;
also 2 Cor. 5:8). John says our hope is that "we shall see Him as
He is" (1 John 3:2). And being with Christ, seeing him as he is,
is the essence of the glory and joy of heaven.

In seeing Christ, we will have the beatific vision of God that
is promised to the pure in heart (Matt. 5:8).[2] Our vision of God
will be in seeing Christ, and it must be, for Christ is the Mediator
between God and man (1 Tim. 2:5), the one through whom we
receive all the blessings and promises of God (2 Cor. 1:20). And
the promise of all promises is God himself, his presence with us,

2. Our vision of God in Christ in heaven is called *beatific* because seeing
him transforms us and gives us "perfect rest and blessedness." See John Owen,
Meditations and Discourses on the Glory of Christ, reprinted in *The Works of John
Owen*, ed. William H. Goold, 24 vols. (Edinburgh: Johnstone & Hunter,
1850–1855; reprint by Banner of Truth Trust, 1965, 1991), 1:413.

our union and communion with him (Gen. 15:1; Heb. 11:6). It is what we lost in the garden, was restored by Christ, and will be ours forever through him.

Believe it. Long for his appearing. Believe it or not, he longs for us to be with him.

Now and Then

This future glory works its way backward into our lives now. We were made for this ultimate purpose: to see God in Christ and by seeing him to know happiness and be transformed. That destiny shapes and orders our lives now. We experience a continuity between now and then: we taste and preview that final vision now, adjusting our eyes to the light, preparing to see him face-to-face then. Seeing Christ now is the cream of spiritual mindedness and honey to the devoted mind.

In 2 Corinthians 3, Paul describes a preview of that final vision that we have now. In his discussion of the relative greatness of the New Covenant over the Old, he alludes to God's appearing to Moses, where "the LORD descended in the cloud and stood with him there" (Ex. 34:5). Moses immediately bows his head and worships (v. 8). God's glory spreads to Moses, so that his face shines when he comes down the mountain. But his shining face unnerves the people, so he takes a veil for their sake.

What Moses experienced is unimaginable. Yet Paul says that we, instead of being like the people who couldn't bear to look at Moses because of the glory, are like Moses. Paul says that when we turn to the Lord, "the veil is taken away" (2 Cor. 3:16), just as "whenever Moses went in before the LORD to speak with Him, he would take the veil off" (Ex. 34:34). Paul makes his point unmistakable: "We all, with unveiled face, beholding as in a mirror the glory of the Lord, are being transformed into the same image from glory to glory, just as by the Spirit of the Lord" (2 Cor. 3:18).

Seeing Christ now "as in a mirror" is not the same as our eventual face-to-face encounter and surely not identical to what Moses experienced on the mountain. Still, like Moses, we see God's glory in Christ now, and his glory changes us. This is the zenith of our spiritual mindedness. It is our mountaintop. To better understand how we see Christ, consider how our vision of him now is like and unlike our vision of him in the end.

The Way We See God Now and Always Is in Christ

We see and know God only because he makes himself known to us. His ultimate self-revelation is in Christ (Heb. 1:1–4), the Word of the Father (John 1:1–3; 14:24). Jesus himself made this clear: "He who has seen Me has seen the Father. . . . Believe Me that I am in the Father and the Father in Me" (John 14:9, 11). We see God in Christ now through his written Word (Luke 24:27); in the end we will see him face to face (1 John 3:2; 1 Cor. 13:12).

We See Christ Now by Faith

In 2 Corinthians 5, Paul says that we long for heaven because we are "absent from the Lord" and in heaven we will be "present with the Lord" (vv. 6, 8). The difference between now and then is that now "we walk by faith," but then "by sight" (v. 7). Our "walk" is our whole relationship to Christ now, which includes our seeing him. Now we see him in his Word as we look by faith.

We See Christ Now by the Mind's Eye

Now we contemplate Christ by our imagination, when it is prompted, led, and directed by the Word and Spirit (1 Cor. 1:23; Gal. 3:1).

We See Christ Now as in a Mirror

Now we gaze on Christ indirectly, "as in a mirror" (2 Cor. 3:18), but then face to face.

We See Christ Now Intermittently

Now we are often prevented from looking on our Beloved by our sin and weakness (Matt. 26:40–41) and the ordinary demands of daily life; our eternal view of him will be uninterrupted.

We See Christ Now Piecemeal

Now our views of Christ are parceled out because of our limitations, so that we see the glory of his meekness in one glance, then the glory of his wisdom in another. Now we cannot take in all his perfections at once (1 Cor. 13:12); but in the end we will see his glory whole, entire, and full.

Our Sight of Christ Now Changes Us Gradually

The sight we have of Christ now spreads his glory to us and changes us into his image, but that change is partial, gradual, and progressive, "from glory to glory" (2 Cor. 3:18). When we see him face to face, the transformation will be immediate and total (1 John 3:2). We will be like him.

Case Study

If I made that sound complicated, perhaps an example of contemplating Christ will pull these elements together and show that it's simpler than my explanation. Suppose we read Luke 12:37, where Jesus says, "Blessed are those servants whom the master, when he comes, will find watching. Assuredly, I say to you that he will gird himself and have them sit down to eat, and will come and serve them."

The image of Christ serving his servants makes us do a double take. It's unexpected. It's upside-down. His abasing himself to turn waiter at the table of unworthy servants is not the way things should be. We think of his majesty and his glory at the right hand of the Father (Acts 2:33). He is Creator (Heb. 1:2), he is Sovereign (Acts 2:36), he is so high above us he stoops down to see us (Ps. 113:4–6). We try to imagine being at his table, yet we know how undeserving we are to be there—the thought of our Lord's serving us overwhelms us (John 13:8). This can't be! Yet Jesus says it's so. Amazed, humbled, stupefied, we bow in worship (Ruth 2:10).

You might recognize that Luke 12:37 lies behind George Herbert's poem at the end of the previous chapter, "Love (III)." The reaction to it that I described follows Herbert's theme. Although most of us can't express ourselves in words that others will read four hundred years from now, we can share Herbert's taste of Love. And our plainspoken-prose reaction to the text has all the elements of our seeing Christ:

- It is an act of faith.
- It is a work of imagination, memory, and reasoning.
- It is based on Scripture and mediated through Scripture.
- It is partial, focusing on only a few of the truths revealed in Christ.
- It is brief and ends too quickly.
- It transforms, at least in shaping the mind and moving the heart (its long-term effects can't be seen in a snapshot).
- We know by faith that the Spirit is at work in this, pouring God's love into our hearts (Rom. 5:5).

This is an encounter with God in Christ. This is spiritual mindedness.

The Regulative Principle of Contemplation

Like Moses, we have unveiled access to God in Christ. But looking on Christ in the Scriptures and using our imagination to see him comes with a risk. It's easy to imagine a Jesus of our own making, a Jesus of superstition or sentimentalism. Suppose, for example, we hear Jesus tell us that he is "gentle" (Matt. 11:29). What does he mean? We need the immediate context to help us to understand, as well as the revelation of Christ in the rest of the Gospels, the Epistles, and the whole Bible. If instead we import an understanding of "gentle" from a Victorian novel, our Jesus might look more like a proper Englishman than the Jesus of the Bible. He might appear very nice, but we would miss the Lord of Glory. The gentleness of the one who is King of Kings and Lord of Lords, the Sustainer of worlds—that is something to contemplate, something that can bring far more comfort when we grasp it, than a nice man.

To see God as he truly is in Christ, we must be guided by the Scriptures. Let it be our lifelong project, then, to know the Scriptures and interpret them well, that we might more and more clearly see Christ as he reveals himself. And let it be our constant practice, when we hear and read the Scriptures, to ask the Spirit who inspired them to teach us (John 14:16, 26; 1 John 2:27). For Christ himself—a sight of him, a taste of his love—is the reason we immerse ourselves in the Scriptures.

Your Face Is Lovely

A taste of his love. I said that because Christ offers himself to us in extraordinary ways:

> Behold, I stand at the door and knock. If anyone hears My voice and opens the door, I will come in to him and dine with him, and he with Me. (Rev. 3:20)

79

If anyone loves Me, he will keep My word; and My Father will love him, and We will come to him and make Our home with him. (John 14:23)

Abide in Me, and I in you. (John 15:4)

He will dine with us? He will make his home with us and in us? This is the language of intimacy, the Beloved with us, the promise of promises. And this seeing Christ by faith in the Word that Paul sets before us in 2 Corinthians 3:18 is the way we open the door and welcome Christ in to dine with us. It is the way we abide in him and he in us. It is a mysterious but very real communion in which the Spirit fills our hearts with the love of God (Rom. 5:5).

What believer would not long for this, seek every day for a taste of his love? Isn't this the one thing we desire of the Lord, the one thing we seek, the *one thing needed* (Ps. 27:4; Luke 10:42)? In seeking Christ in the Word, we hear his knock, we know his voice, we open the door to him, and he comes in (Rev. 3:20; John 10:27).

O my dove, in the clefts of the rock,
In the secret places of the cliff,
Let me see your face,
Let me hear your voice;
For your voice is sweet,
And your face is lovely. (Song 2:14)

Reflection and Praxis

1. If communing with Christ by contemplating or meditating on him is new to you, catechisms may give you specific starting points. Eventually your prompts will come as Christ meets you in his Word—whether in the Gospels, the Epistles, Moses, or

the prophets—but catechisms can help to focus your attention on different aspects of Christ's nature and character, as well as all he did and suffered for us. They are brief summaries but give Scripture references so you can explore further. Each of the catechisms below articulates a historic, biblical understanding of Christ.

- *To Be a Christian*[3] (Anglican), questions and answers 48–83.
- Westminster Shorter Catechism (Presbyterian), questions and answers 21–28.
- Heidelberg Catechism (Reformed), questions and answers 1, 29–52.
- New City Catechism (Reformed Evangelical), questions and answers 1, 20–30.
- Keach's Catechism (Baptist), questions and answers 25–32.
- For some basics on how to meditate, see chapter 8 below, or J. I. Packer and Carolyn Nystrom, *Praying: Finding Our Way through Duty to Delight* (Downers Grove, IL: IVP Books, 2006), 68–96.

2. If we let our thoughts of Christ be guided by something other than Scripture, such as a film or book that takes liberties with the biblical revelation of Christ, what are some distortions we might make? Identify some real harms of this.

3. John Owen spends one-third of his chapter on spiritual thoughts of Christ showing how they strengthen us to bear suffering in a way that glorifies God. I didn't include his points,

---

3. The Anglican Church of North America, *To Be a Christian: An Anglican Catechism* (Wheaton, IL: Crossway, 2020). J. I. Packer was the theological editor for the creation of this catechism.

but his idea is worth exploring, since (as Owen reminds us) we will all suffer. What are some ways that regular meditation on Christ and communion with him help us to face suffering? Cite some Scriptures that support your answer.

4. Hymns and songs that are faithful to the Scriptures can prompt our thoughts of Christ and stir our hearts. Choose one of the following and reflect on it (and sing it) every day for a week. Make some notes about how it shapes your communion with him.

- "Savior of the Nations, Come," Ambrose of Milan (340–397)
- "Of the Father's Love Begotten," Aurelius Clemens Prudentius (348–413)
- "When Christ's Appearing Was Made Known," Cælis Sedulius, fifth century
- "O Lord of Light, Who Made the Stars," Latin hymn, ninth century
- "All Glory, Laud, and Honor," Theodulph of Orleans, c. 820
- "O Sacred Head, Now Wounded," Bernard of Clairvaux (1091–1153)
- "Jesus, Thou Joy of Loving Hearts," Bernard of Clairvaux (1091–1153)
- "O Come, O Come, Emmanuel," Latin, twelfth century
- "Once He Came in Blessing," Johann Horn (c. 1490–1547)
- "How Lovely Shines the Morning Star," Philipp Niccolai, 1597
- "Ah, Holy Jesus, How Hast Thou Offended," Johann Heermann, 1630
- "Jesus, Priceless Treasure," Johann Franck, 1655
- "What Wondrous Love Is This," American folk hymn
- "Glory Be to Jesus," Italian, eighteenth century

- "I Know That My Redeemer Lives," Samuel Medley (1738–1799)
- "Come, Thou Fount of Every Blessing," Robert Robinson, 1758
- "How Sweet the Name of Jesus Sounds," John Newton, 1779
- "Jesus, Thy Blood and Righteousness," Nikolaus Ludwig von Zinzendorf, 1739
- "At the Name of Jesus," Caroline M. Noel, 1870
- "Before the Throne of God Above," Charitie L. de Chenez (1841–1923)

5. The names of the Son of God can also prompt our thoughts of him and stir our hearts. Choose one of the following and reflect on it every day for a week. Make some notes about how it shapes your communion with him.

- Advocate (1 John 2:1–2)
- Bread of God (John 6:33)
- Deliverer (Rom. 11:26)
- High Priest (Heb. 3:1)
- Good Shepherd (John 10:11)
- Immanuel (Matt. 1:23)
- King of Kings (1 Tim. 6:15)
- Lamb of God (John 1:29)
- Mediator (1 Tim. 2:5)
- Physician (Luke 4:23)
- Prince of Peace (Isa. 9:6)
- The True Vine (John 15:1)
- The Way (John 14:6)
- Wisdom (1 Cor. 1:30)

Suggestions for Further Reading

Justin S. Holcomb's *God with Us: 365 Devotions on the Person and Work of Christ* (Minneapolis: Bethany House, 2021) isn't a systematic approach to Christology but builds our knowledge of him through 365 one-page readings of Scripture and related comments by devotional masters from every era of church history. John Owen's magisterial *Meditations and Discourses on the Glory of Christ*, reprinted in *The Works of John Owen*, ed. William H. Goold, 24 vols. (Edinburgh: Johnstone & Hunter, 1850–1855; reprint by Banner of Truth Trust, 1965, 1991), 1:273–461, is well worth the challenge; Owen's work has been abridged and made easy to read by R. J. K. Law, *The Glory of Christ* (Edinburgh: The Banner of Truth Trust, 1994); I've also adapted Owen's work on Christ in *The Glorious Christ: Meditations on His Person, Work, and Love* (Phillipsburg, NJ: P&R Publishing, 2023). And Jonty Rhodes shows how theology can (and should) be clear and devotional in *Man of Sorrows, King of Glory: What the Humiliation and Exaltation of Jesus Mean for Us* (Wheaton, IL: Crossway, 2021).

6

the devoted mind
seeks the face of God

*Let imagination range to what you may suppose is God's
utmost limit, and you will find Him present there; strain as
you will there is always a further horizon towards which to
strain. Infinity is His property, just as the power of making
such effort is yours. Words will fail you, but His being will
not be circumscribed.*
—Hilary of Poitiers

*Now what is more wonderful than the divine beauty, what
thought more alluring than the splendour of God?*
—Basil of Caesarea

The Meaning of Everything in Three Prepositions

What is the meaning of life? Some say love, others say
happiness; the ancients say it's finding the truth, the moderns
say making your own truth; some say it's found in creating
beauty, others say in appreciating the beautiful, the true, and the
good; some say it's striving for the greatest wisdom and virtue,

others the highest pleasure; some say it's living your dream, others say serving society; some say it's being true to yourself, others say it's being faithful to friends; some say meaning can only be found in community, others say only in solitude and contemplation; some say it can't be found without risk and pushing yourself beyond your limits, others deny this and say it can't be found except by achieving tranquility and balance; some say meaning is found by the profoundest thought, others by the deepest feelings, still others by the bravest acts of will; some deny there is any meaning and say therefore that we are nothings going nowhere.

But Paul shows us a more excellent way.

After he plumbs the depths of the gospel (Rom. 1–8) and scales the heights of God's secret will (Rom. 9–11), Paul is beside himself. He uncorks his *O altitudo!* and pours forth a bottle of bubbling praise of God's wisdom and knowledge that, it turns out, can't be measured (Rom. 11:33–36).[1] Unable to press further, Paul gives the summing-up statement to end all summing-up statements:

> For of Him and through Him and to Him are all things, to whom be glory forever. Amen. (Rom. 11:36)

Each of the prepositions in that sentence carries a hefty payload.

Of	All things are "of Him": everything that exists has its source in our Triune God's power and pleasure.	Gen. 1:1; Job 38:4–7; Ps. 33:6; Isa. 45:18; John 1:1–3; Col. 1:16; Heb. 11:3; Rev. 4:11

---

1. Remember from chapter 5 that *O altitudo!* are the first words of Romans 11:33 in the Latin Vulgate.

Through	All things are "through Him": everything that exists is sustained by our Triune God's power and pleasure, and everything that happens is governed by his wisdom and will.	Gen. 45:5–8; Deut. 8:11–18; Ps. 104; Prov. 16:9; Matt. 10:29–30; Acts 17:28; Col. 1:17; Phil. 4:19; Heb. 1:3; James 1:17
To	All things are "to him": everything that exists and happens redounds to our Triune God's glory, as Paul punctuates his praise, "to whom be glory forever."	1 Chron. 29:11; Phil. 4:20; 1 Tim. 1:17; 1 Peter 4:11; Rev. 5:13

Amen.

This is the meaning of life. All things are of, through, and to him, so he is "all in all" (Eph. 1:23). And when God reveals himself as our meaning, it shapes the thoughts of the spiritual mind. Who or what else could compete to be the supreme object of our thoughts and desires? What are our thoughts of heaven but thoughts of God's home? What are our thoughts of Christ but thoughts of God in his Son, the Mediator who shows us God? What are our thoughts of creation but thoughts of God's "invisible attributes" made visible in the display of his "eternal power and Godhead" (Rom. 1:20)?

And what are our thoughts of God but our source of purest pleasure?

Delight and Its Consequents

The devoted mind delights to think of God. Thoughts of him rejoice and refresh the hearts of his people and stir them to gratitude.

Sing praise to the LORD, you saints of His,
And give thanks at the remembrance of His holy name.
(Ps. 30:4)

Thoughts of God begin with what he is—his infinite, eternal, and unchangeable perfections. Paul tells us to meditate on "whatever things are noble, whatever things are just, whatever things are pure, whatever things are lovely, whatever things are of good report, if there is any virtue and if there is anything praiseworthy" (Phil. 4:8), and God is the over-brimming fountain of all these—and more. He is holy, wise, just, powerful, gracious, merciful, and generous. All that is good and beautiful flows from him, for he is the spring of all goodness and beauty. He is love and all loveliness. And there is no limit to any of these excellencies in him.

Because God is all in all and the sum of all good, when we feel that our hearts are like a faded leaf or a broken bowl, or our souls are parched, or life is slipping away, thoughts of God in his perfections renew, refresh, and restore us. We "taste and see" the goodness of God in our thoughts of him (Ps. 34:8). When we delight in him, we have a strong assurance that "this God"—this holy, powerful, just, good, and gracious God—is "our God forever and ever; he will be our guide even to death" (Ps. 48:14). And our delight in thoughts of him tells us we are born of his Spirit, because his Spirit in us delights in him and is our foretaste of our eternal delight in him through Christ.

Rejoice with Trembling

Thoughts of God that delight both him and the devoted mind have a unique timbre, a quality that seems out of place in our world. A recent translator of Brother Lawrence feels that his "images for God" have "autocratic associations with seventeenth-century structures of inequity," so she renders his "Lord" and "Master" as "Friend" and "Teacher."[2] Her choices are extreme but not surprising. In our society, reverence has long been passé. Our commitment to egalitarianism has led to a decades-long purge of all that suggests inequality of honor, status, authority, or power. That includes honorific titles, expressions of respect such as "yes, ma'am," and other verbal and nonverbal demonstrations of courtesy. Old-school manners are in exile.

Some of this is harmless cultural drift. But not all. When it spills over into our worship, it atrophies our devotion. Worship that never rises above a casual familiarity suggests small thoughts of God. When "Hallowed be Thy name" no longer marks our prayers and thoughts of God, we have fallen from true piety.

Regardless of how feudal or democratic our society is, our relationship with God has a quality that goes against the grain. It's a paradoxical quality that can only be maintained by faith and love. Two exhortations from Hebrews placed side by side show what I mean:

| Let us therefore come *boldly* to the throne of grace, that we may obtain mercy and find grace to help in time of need. (4:16) | Let us offer to God acceptable worship, with *reverence* and *awe*, for our God is a consuming fire. (12:28–29 ESV) |

Which is it? Should we approach God boldly or with reverence and awe? Yes. Both. At the same time. Psalm 2 unites these

2. Nicholas Herman, Brother Lawrence of the Resurrection, *Practice of the Presence: A Revolutionary Translation by Carmen Acevedo Butcher* (Minneapolis: Broadleaf Books, 2022), 34.

two poles and tells us to "rejoice with trembling" (v. 11). This is acceptable worship. How is this possible?

Fear, trembling, reverence, and awe should be second nature to us. If we look at God as he is revealed to us in the Bible and in nature—in his infinite greatness, infinite holiness, and infinite power—and then look at ourselves, the difference is obvious. We are undone. And yet, at the same time, seeing his glory and beauty evokes from us praise, wonder, rejoicing, delight that can hardly be endured—and draws us toward him.

> When Solomon had finished praying, fire came down from heaven and consumed the burnt offering and the sacrifices; and the glory of the LORD filled the temple. And the priests could not enter the house of the LORD, because the glory of the LORD had filled the LORD's house. When all the children of Israel saw how the fire came down, and the glory of the LORD on the temple, they bowed their faces to the ground on the pavement, and worshiped and praised the LORD, saying:
>
> > "For He is good,
> > For His mercy endures forever." (2 Chron. 7:1–3)

Our upbringing may have prepared us for reverence, or we may never have seen it expressed. Boldness may come naturally to our personality, or we may shrink from intimacy. Some of us wake up smiling, and others of us were born grumpy old men. Still, to offer acceptable worship, each of us must grow into that bold-and-reverent, rejoicing-and-trembling posture before God. How each of us grows will look different, depending on our faith and gifts, what we have by nature and what we have from the Spirit. But grow we must.

God Is

The devoted mind is convinced that thoughts of God are its source of purest pleasure. Thus it comes to God boldly and reverently, rejoicing and trembling. And what does it think about? Our first thoughts of God are that he exists. Now don't rush past this, taking his existence for granted. The writer of Hebrews spells out step 1, so let's not skip it: "But without faith it is impossible to please Him, for he who comes to God must believe that He is, and that He is a rewarder of those who diligently seek Him" (Heb. 11:6).

Believing "that He is" doesn't go without saying. God first reveals himself to Moses as "I AM" (Ex. 3:14). It's our first article of faith. Millions of believers around the world reaffirm each Sunday, "I believe in God the Father Almighty." It is good and right to do so, and we should proclaim those words with reverence and awe, rejoicing and trembling. It is good and right because it honors and pleases God, and because it is "the shield of faith with which [we] will be able to quench all the fiery darts of the wicked one" (Eph. 6:16). One of his fiery darts is atheism.

"Philosophical atheism" sounds out of place in a list of pop-culture phenomena. Although it's nothing new (Ps. 14:1), some years ago it took a brief turn as the in thing. Atheist intellectuals achieved celebrity, topped bestseller lists, appeared on talk shows, and debated champions of religion on campuses in packed lecture halls. They were bold, not settling to argue for freedom of thought but charging that religion was not only wishful thinking but a ruinous evil.

Atheism is no longer a fad, but it remains a force. And though we may feel confident and unshakable in our faith today, we shouldn't be naive. Our Western culture is secular; as a society, we no longer draw on God to explain reality. Belief in him is no longer dominant; most think it's no longer tenable or even plausible. Those who believe in him are more and more the ones who must justify their belief to skeptics who are convinced they have reason and science on their side.

This plays into Satan's modus operandi. In the garden, he asked questions to sow seeds of doubt in Eve. "Has God indeed said?" (Gen. 3:1). From time to time, his simple questions will come to mind: *Is there really a God? How do you know? Aren't you arrogant to be so sure?* When those questions come, don't linger over them. Dismiss Satan in Jesus's name and words: "Away with you, Satan! For it is written, 'You shall worship the LORD your God, and Him only you shall serve'" (Matt. 4:10). And keep him away by asking the Spirit to seal your faith with his truth: "I believe in God the Father Almighty." If questions or even doubts about God's existence persist, reinforce your faith by reviewing a defense of God's existence.[3]

Frequent thoughts of God's existence also prepare us to bear witness to the secular world:

> Let all the nations be gathered together,
> And let the people be assembled.
> . . . .
> Let them bring out their witnesses, that they may be justified;
> Or let them hear and say, "It is truth."
> "You are My witnesses," says the LORD,
> "And My servant whom I have chosen,
> That you may know and believe Me,
> And understand that I am He.
> Before Me there was no God formed,
> Nor shall there be after Me.
> I, even I, am the LORD,

3. I will list a few titles in the suggestions for reading at the end of the chapter. Consider also talking to your pastor or mentor about your questions.

And besides Me there is no savior.
I have declared and saved,
I have proclaimed,
And there was no foreign god among you;
Therefore you are My witnesses,"
Says the LORD, "that I am God." (Isa. 43:9–12)

Without that witness, there's no hope for the world.

No Little Thoughts

Although it's true that the devoted mind delights in thoughts of God, it can't help being overwhelmed. God's infinite, eternal, and unchangeable existence quickly runs us past the limits of language. Our minds tire and falter. Thinking of God's infinite existence and perfections feels like staring at the sun, and we want to turn away. But this exhaustion serves a holy purpose; it puts us in our place and italicizes the ineffable glory of our God. So although we might fittingly ask God to forgive the smallness of our thoughts of him, we also thank him that he won't fit inside our minds. If he could, who could worship him?

It can also be tempting to dismiss what we can't fathom as irrelevant or even impossible. But humility before God cultivates a holy admiration of what we cannot comprehend. And I hope you already know that we comprehend nothing about God. That isn't to say we don't know anything about him, but what we know is infinitesimally small compared to what we don't know. Our capacity is limited. We have a thimble; he's an ocean. If we fill our thimble with water from the ocean, it's truly ocean water, but there's so much more out there. So we rightly say that we know that God is good, because he reveals himself as good in his Word and in his dealings with us. But we will never be able to grasp the fullness of his goodness. And that's a good thing.

Thinking of God's *omnipresence* and *omniscience* protects and feeds our souls. Not just knowing as fact that he is everywhere and that nothing escapes his notice, but often reflecting on what that means, is especially effective against certain temptations. Each of us learns through painful experience that we can't be around certain people without being pulled into their mocking or rowdiness or cliquishness.[4] Paul, like Proverbs, was clear: "Do not be misled: 'Bad company corrupts good character'" (1 Cor. 15:33 NIV). A front-burner awareness that we live *coram deo*—before the face of God—can strengthen our resolve to decline their invitations. And we learn, also by trial and error, that nothing good can happen in certain places at certain times of day (Eph. 5:12). But the darkness is not dark to God, whether in a dark alley or on the dark web (Ps. 139:12). Let thoughts of his ever-present light steer us away from dark dangers.

The fact that God is with us and knows us doesn't only teach us to say no to ungodliness: it comforts us in times of unwelcome solitude. When we are alone with our thoughts, our natural loneliness can stray into self-pity; if we nurse that self-pity, we can find ourselves bitter, even toward God. Or we can indulge unhealthy fantasies to take our minds off the hurt and boredom. David's thoughts in the watches of the night reveal a counterstrategy:

I will bless the LORD who has given me counsel;
My heart also instructs me in the night seasons. (Ps. 16:7)

What was his heart lecturing him on as he lay awake on his bed? The doctrine of God's omnipresence:

4. C. S. Lewis often reflected on the temptation of "The Inner Ring." See his essay by that title in various collections, including C. S. Lewis, *They Asked for a Paper* (London: Geoffrey Bles, 1962), 139–49. He explores the temptation more fully in the character of Mark Studdock in *That Hideous Strength* (New York: Macmillan Publishing Co., 1946).

I have set the LORD always before me;
Because He is at my right hand I shall not be moved. (Ps. 16:8)

Not everyone is comfortable with solitude; even the most die-hard homebodies weary of extended isolation. Not only are midnight meditations like David's a salve for our lonely hearts, but they restore us to reverence and awe and boldness and joy in God's presence. They enable us to say with Jesus, "I am not alone, because the Father is with Me" (John 16:32).

God's *omnipotence* will have pride of place in the thoughts of a devoted mind, for if God is not all-powerful, "we are of all men the most pitiable" (1 Cor. 15:19). If he is not all-powerful, how can we be certain of his promises? If he is not all-powerful, how can we hope in the resurrection? If he is not all-powerful, how can we keep our sanity in a world that edges every day closer to self-destruction?

But we are assured not only that God is faithful in his covenant love to his people but that he has the power to save them from their sins, from Satan, and from the world:

Once God has spoken;
   twice have I heard this:
that power belongs to God,
   and that to you, O Lord, belongs steadfast love.
   (Ps. 62:11–12 ESV)

God's eternal existence, omnipresence, omniscience, and omnipotence are too much for our small minds, but they are only the beginning. Our lifelong project as lovers of God is to learn to swim in the ocean of his being and beauty; then not only will we know where we came from and where we are going, who we are and why we are here, but we will have the ineffable joy of communion with our all-in-all God.

Reflection and Praxis

1. Thinking about reverence before God in the context of the casual and even irreverent trends of our culture, take stock of your soul's posture before God. Consider the way you address God as well as the way you talk about him. What happens in your heart when you hear his name praised in worship or abused on the streets? Think about your engagement in worship and how God-directed your heart is. Think about your private prayers and meditation. Are you reckoning with God's holiness?

If what you learn about yourself makes you want to deepen your reverence toward God, where can you start? What distractions do you need to set aside? What body postures might help?[5] What preparations? What disciplines?

If you have a mentor or close spiritual friend, talk through this together.

2. Owen's concern in his culture was that *formality* in worship undermines reverence. *Informality* today can be a barrier for us. How can each work against reverence?

3. As you think about ways to grow in reverence toward God, think about how you show respect and honor in your human relationships. Could some of those help to train you in reverence? Think of how you show respect while listening to others (for example, with your body language) and when speaking to others (for example, in the dignity and thoughtfulness of your expression). Are there any transferable lessons?

---

5. "As for the bodily gestures customarily observed in praying, such as kneeling and uncovering the head, they are exercises whereby we try to rise to a greater reverence for God." John Calvin, *Institutes*, 3.20.33.

4. Besides our thoughts of God's existence and nature, we delight to think of and admire his character. Below are some attributes of God. Choose one and review the Scripture references listed with it. Try to understand the quality and think of a few implications (for example, "If God is sovereign over all things, I can feel safe when our society feels like it is collapsing"). Write a brief prayer that praises God for being who he is.

God is . . .

Sovereign	Ex. 15:18; Pss. 46:8–10; 103:19; 115:1–3; 135:6; Isa. 40:21–26; Dan. 4:34–35; Matt. 6:10; Rev. 5:12–14
Eternal	1 Chron. 29:10–13; Ps. 90:2; Isa. 9:6–7; 57:15; Dan. 7:14; Deut. 33:27; 1 Tim. 1:17; 6:16; Heb. 1:8; Rev. 1:8
Immutable	Num. 23:19; Pss. 102:26–28; 119:89–96; Mal. 3:6; Heb. 13:8; James 1:17
Omnipresent	Jer. 23:23–24; Pss. 23:4; 33:13–15; 139:5–9; 1 Kings 8:27; Acts 17:24–28
Omniscient	Pss. 94:8–11; 139:17–18; 147:5; Isa. 40:27–28; Rom. 11:33
Love	Deut. 7:7–8; Isa. 54:10; John 3:16; 13:1; Rom. 5:8; 8:37–39; Gal. 2:20; 1 John 3:16; 4:7–16
Wise	Job 9:4; 28:1–28; Ps. 104:24; Prov. 8; Rom. 11:33–36; 16:27
Omnipotent	Ex. 15:1–18; Job 26:14; 38:1–41:34; Ps. 62:11; 115:1–3; Isa. 40:17, 23, 24; Jer. 32:17; Luke 1:37; Rev. 19:1
Holy	Ex. 15:11; Lev. 19:2; 1 Sam. 2:2; 1 Chron. 16:29; Pss. 99:3; 110:3; Isa. 6:3–5; Rev. 4:8

5. How can thinking specifically of God's omnipotence help us in times of hard providence (see chapter 3)? Consider these passages to help you reflect: 2 Kings 6:15–17, Daniel 3:17–18, and 2 Timothy 4:17 (where Paul is waiting to face Nero).

Suggestions for Further Reading

Jen Wilkin's *None Like Him: 10 Ways God Is Different from Us (and Why That's a Good Thing)* (Wheaton, IL: Crossway, 2016) is justly my wife's favorite book. Matthew Barrett's *None Greater: The Undomesticated Attributes of God* (Grand Rapids: Baker Books, 2019) is another accessible yet meaty way to get to know God's attributes. The unsurpassed Puritan masterpiece on the doctrine of God is Stephen Charnock, *The Existence and Attributes of God*, available in a new edition edited by Mark Jones (Wheaton, IL: Crossway, 2022). An old writer who modeled humility and wonder in his theology, addressing his work to God as a prayer, is Anselm of Canterbury, *Proslogion* (eleventh century). Timothy Keller, *The Reason for God: Belief in an Age of Skepticism* (New York: Dutton, 2008) presents solid reasons for believing in God, and R.C. Sproul, *Does God Exist?* (Orlando: Reformation Trust, 2019) is brief yet addresses the main issues.

Part 2

inclination and satisfaction

7

the devoted mind
is devoted

God cannot be known except by devotion.
—HILARY OF POITIERS

Don't Let John Owen Scare You

After all this talk about thoughts of the Beloved, you may be thinking, "My soul thirsts for God, for the living God. *When can I go and meet with God?*" (Ps. 42:2 NIV). Or maybe all this talk about thoughts of the Beloved has already "brought [you] to the banqueting house" (Song 2:4) and you are delighting in him now and wish I would stop talking. Or maybe you'd like to fling this book across the room, because it's aggravating an old wound: You picked it up because you long for thoughts of the Beloved with an inconsolable ache. But, if you're like me, when you get an idea of something lovely about Christ and try to think of it, before you can form a complete thought your mind flits away like a bat after a mosquito.

Our frustration is unavoidable because we were made to contemplate and commune with our God. We won't be happy—won't have the fullness of life and peace—till we see him. As Paul says, "He who has prepared us for this very thing is God" (2 Cor. 5:5). "This very thing" is what we "groan" for, "earnestly desiring to be clothed with our habitation which is from heaven" (v. 2), because until then "we are absent from the Lord" (v. 6). By his grace and for the time being, God "has given us the Spirit as a guarantee" (v. 5). And, as we have seen, the Spirit is the source of our thoughts of heaven, of God, of Christ. These thoughts are our consolation, our combat rations, if you will, until we are "clothed with our habitation which is from heaven."

But there is a discipline of the devoted mind that can turn our combat rations into a feast. In a single chapter, John Owen calls it "stated meditation" and "spiritual meditation" and "heavenly meditation" and "holy meditation" and "designed meditations" and "solemn meditation" and "stated spiritual meditation" and "holy, fixed meditations."[1] He needs all those adjectives to give proper weight to what he means by meditation. Owen says it's hard work, and even says that some people can't do it. I prefer to think of meditation as something that grows with us: just as babies can learn to dog paddle and stay afloat in the pool, even baby believers can learn the basics of meditation; and, as children mature and add new strokes to their swimming skills each summer, with discipline everyone can deepen their meditation. But Owen is right that meditation is demanding. Few of us will be masters of meditation, just as few of us will be Olympian swimmers. But because the prize is the Pearl, a devoted mind won't be put off by the work.

---

1. See chapter 10 of *The Grace and Duty of Being Spiritually Minded*, 1681, reprinted in *The Works of John Owen*, ed. William H. Goold, 24 vols. (Edinburgh: Johnstone & Hunter, 1850–1855; reprint by Banner of Truth Trust, 1965, 1991), 7:379–94.

Three Powers of the Soul

The seventeenth century was a golden age of interest and instruction in meditation, from Francis de Sales and the Counter-Reformation through Joseph Hall and the Anglicans to Richard Baxter and the Puritans.[2] Although they differed in details of methodology, all the old masters said the essentials of meditation corresponded to what they called the three powers of the soul: *memory, understanding,* and *will.*[3] We can map what they said onto a simple and familiar framework.

Bible Reading Is the Work of the Memory in Meditation

As we read the Scriptures or hear them read, our imagination fixes the content of the text in our minds and moves it to the front burner. Depending on the text, we might picture a nervous Nicodemus making his way from shadow to shadow to meet Jesus under cover of darkness, or Goliath towering over and taunting David, or Paul meeting Lydia at the river; we might imagine the sick wrenching in David's gut when he hears Nathan's "Thou art

2. For a comparison of de Sales, Baxter, and Owen, see J. I. Packer, "Seventeenth-century Teaching on the Christian Life—1: An Introduction to some Puritan and Roman Moral Theology," *The Churchman* 71, no. 4 (Oct.–Dec. 1957): 166–73; part 2 of the essay is in *The Churchman* 72, no. 1 (Jan.–Mar. 1958): 23–29.

3. See Louis L. Martz, *The Poetry of Meditation* (New Haven and London: Yale University Press, revised edition 1962). Martz doesn't discuss Owen, but Owen's definition of meditation follows the pattern Martz describes: "By solemn or stated meditation, I intend the thoughts of some subject spiritual and divine, with the fixing, forcing, and ordering of our thoughts about it, with a design to affect our own hearts and souls with the matter of it, or the things contained in it. By this design it is distinguished from the study of the word, wherein our principal aim is to learn the truth, or to declare it unto others; and so also from prayer, whereof God himself is the immediate object. But in meditation it is the affecting of our own hearts and minds with love, delight, and humiliation." See *The Works of John Owen*, 7:384.

the man" or the furious, indignant faces of the Pharisees when Jesus calls them a "brood of vipers"; or we might trace and note the themes of Paul's page-long sentence that opens his letter to the church in Ephesus.

Bible Study Is the Work of the Understanding in Meditation

Now that we have the content clearly in mind, we process it. We analyze it, connect it to its context, recall other places in Scripture that cover the same theme or event. We draw conclusions about what it says about God's character and power and beauty. We search to see how it shows Christ and our need for him. We ask what it says about human nature or our relation to creation, about how to worship God or how to live when surrounded by unbelievers. Whether we do this informally and intuitively, or we apply a sophisticated hermeneutical method, we are using our minds to search out the meaning of what God says. But not as an end in itself; if we stop here, we haven't meditated.[4]

Bible Appropriation Is the Work of the Will in Meditation

I'm using the familiar term "appropriation" (or "application"), but I need to specify what that means in terms of meditation. The old masters understood the will to include not just our resolve to act but our *affections*. I've used that word already, but it's archaic and its meaning may not be clear. In the simplest sense, affections are the inclinations of the heart—leaning *toward* something desirable and leaning *away from* anything repellant. Affections are "motions" deep inside us that are evoked by the understanding, by reflection. When the understanding examines

---

4. "I call it the acting of *all* the powers of the soul to difference it from the common meditation of students, which is usually the mere employment of the brain. . . . The understanding is not the whole soul, and therefore cannot do the whole work." Richard Baxter, *The Saints' Everlasting Rest*, ed. John T. Wilkinson (Vancouver, British Columbia: Regent College Publishing, 2004), 142.

something and judges it beautiful, the heart delights in it, and that delight is an affection.[5]

The Three Powers at Work

Holy love is the chief affection and the fountain of all godly affections,[6] such as desire, hope, joy, gratitude, and contentedness. What makes those affections godly is what evokes them. Desire is godly when we desire God and what God desires. Hope is godly when it rises from reflection on God's promises. Gratitude is godly when it flows from recognizing God's generosity to us. Negative affections such as hatred, anger, and grief can also be godly: when we hate sin and grieve over it because we feel its offense to God, God is pleased.

We cultivate the connection from the understanding to the affections by what Richard Baxter called "Soliloquy" or self-preaching, following the pattern in the Psalms:

Why are you cast down, O my soul?
And why are you disquieted within me?
Hope in God, for I shall yet praise Him
For the help of His countenance. (Pss. 42:5, 11; 43:5)

Bless the LORD, O my soul;
And all that is within me, bless His holy name!

5. Theologians throughout church history have defined the affections and, as Jonathan Edwards admitted, "It must be confessed, that language is here somewhat imperfect, and the meaning of words in a considerable measure loose and unfixed." Edwards, *Religious Affections*, ed. John E. Smith, vol. 2, *The Works of Jonathan Edwards* (New Haven: Yale University Press, 1959), 96–99. The definition I give is simplified and useful for our purposes, but not intended to be comprehensive.

6. See Jonathan Edwards, *Religious Affections*, 106; Thomas Aquinas, *Summa Theologiae*, I–II, 62, 4.

Bless the LORD, O my soul,
And forget not all His benefits:
Who forgives all your iniquities,
Who heals all your diseases,
Who redeems your life from destruction,
Who crowns you with lovingkindness and tender mercies,
Who satisfies your mouth with good things,
So that your youth is renewed like the eagle's. (Ps. 103:1–5)

David reflects on God's help and calls his heart to hope. He thinks of God's forgiveness and healing and generosity and salvation and stirs his whole soul to praise him. In his musing he talks to himself, but he talks to himself in the presence of God, attending to God his Beloved.

This relationship between the understanding and the affections might sound familiar. In the introduction, I suggested that we think of the work of the devoted mind in three modes: *contemplation*, *inclination*, and *satisfaction*. In the last several chapters, we've surveyed ways to contemplate our Beloved. The *inclination* toward God that marks a spiritual mind grows from that contemplation of him.

For example, suppose you read the account of the crucifixion in John's gospel, and you pause over the words of Pilate, "I find no fault in him" (19:4). You have the scene in your memory. You think about connections to the Passover, the need for the spotless lamb, the priest inspecting the animal and declaring it a fitting offering. This triggers a chain of thinking about Christ and his innocence, his suffering in your place. This leads you to recall Paul's comments about the one who knew no sin and yet became sin so that we might become the righteousness of God (2 Cor. 5:21). In your soliloquy, you call your heart to *wonder* at Christ's humility and love, *grieve* over your sin, *marvel* that the religious leaders hated Jesus so much. As you muse, the fire burns

(Ps. 39:3); your affections are warmed and incline you to other acts of the will: repentance, resolve, appeals to God for grace to live a life worthy of Christ's sacrifice (Phil. 1:27).

This chapter isn't a full course in meditation. My goal is modest: to ensure that we don't settle for a mere intellectual grasp of our Beloved. Communion with him is the longing of our hearts—to taste his love, enjoy his beauty. Meditation is our means not only of getting to know him better but of vigorously drawing our hearts toward him in love. So we pray with George Herbert, as we approach God's Word, that we will never be satisfied with mere knowledge:

> Nay, I will read thy book, and never move
> Till I have found therein thy love.[7]

It's about Time

If I told you that you could reach your optimal body weight and be physically fit in one month by eating whatever your heart desires and never moving from your hammock, I would lose all credibility with you. I hope that I would likewise lose credibility if I gave you the impression that being spiritually minded is similarly effortless. Remember Owen's title: *The Grace and Duty of Being Spiritually Minded*. God in his grace creates new life in us, gives us his Spirit, plants a hunger in us to know him. From the foundation of his generosity he calls us, in the words of Paul to Timothy, to "fan into flame the gift of God" (2 Tim. 1:6 ESV).

Over several chapters, we've seen something of what it means to fan God's gift into the flame of spiritual mindedness. But one thing required isn't a skill or technique or matter of training or advanced theological studies. It's time. It's time devoted to setting

---

7. George Herbert, "The Thanksgiving," lines 45–46.

our minds on God, to meditating on him, to communing with him. And our unwillingness to set aside time for communion with God is, for many people, the primary reason we enjoy little of the life and peace of spiritual mindedness.

When I catalogued the phrases Owen uses to describe meditation, I noticed that a few of them contain the word *stated*. Stated meditations are meditations at a set time. Any experienced believer will tell you that if you don't have a set or stated time that you devote to meditation, it simply won't happen. That's why our first, simplest step toward meditation is often the hardest.

1. Commit to God a Regular Devoted Time

Choose a time and place you can protect from distractions and interruptions, even if it means withdrawing into the wilderness like Jesus did (Luke 5:16). Choose a time when you are alert and fresh. David might have been a night person (Ps. 63:6), but Jesus slipped away to commune with the Father before daylight (Mark 1:35). Make this time precious, a treasure you guard with your life. If you devote your time to God and draw near to him, he will draw near to you (James 4:8). It will be precious indeed.

2. Prepare Your Mind and Heart as a Fragrant Offering

This is a time to cultivate the reverence for God we talked about in the previous chapter. As the writer of Ecclesiastes puts it, "Let not your heart utter anything hastily before God. For God is in heaven, and you on earth" (5:2). Perhaps start with a brief prayer asking God to remind you of his greatness as your Creator, or his limitless power, or his universal presence. Ask him to fill your heart with awe that he would take notice of you (Ps. 8:4) and that the Holy One of Glory would invite you into his presence (Heb. 10:22).

3. Ascend from Duty through Discipline to Delight

Setting aside time every day, protecting that time, composing your mind and heart, seeking the Spirit's help, reading the text, figuring out what God is saying, inclining your heart according to God's Word—you might feel like you're standing at the base of Kilimanjaro and your backpack is already pulling you down. You want the view from the top but you're not so sure you're up to the climb. Alas, no climb, no view.

However, the path up this mountain, though often steep and sometimes hard to follow, is lined with springs and vistas that reward and refresh the devoted climber. These are the tastes of God himself in Christ, the glimpses of the beauty of his character and his perfections, the sweet reassurances of his love as we remember his suffering and death for us, the reinvigorating of our hope in his promises and our longing to be forever with our Beloved. If we begin the ascent of meditation out of a sense of hope and holy duty, if we push through dry times by discipline in dependence on God, we will not be disappointed but will break through to delight.

> You will show me the path of life;
> In Your presence is fullness of joy;
> At Your right hand are pleasures forevermore. (Ps. 16:11)

Pushing Through and Pressing On

Hezekiah's description of his prayers during his sickness are a sobering image of a frustrated soul:

> Like a crane or a swallow, so I chattered;
> I mourned like a dove;
> My eyes fail from looking upward.
> O Lord, I am oppressed;
> Undertake for me! (Isa. 38:14)

Our thoughts will often be broken and our prayers will be like bird-chatter. Sometimes our meditation won't rise higher than a fresh sense of our weakness and insufficiency. What then?

Cry and Sigh to God for Help and Relief

Sometimes we grieve over the darkness and instability of our minds. If we sense our weakness and wandering and turn to God for strength and direction, we are drawing close to him even in that. This too is seeking God's face. We are leaning and depending on him, learning again that apart from him we can do nothing.

When Thoughts Scatter, Shoot Arrow Prayers

Sometimes we can't stay focused for even three seconds. That's a call to imitate Hezekiah and aim a short and sharp prayer—an arrow prayer—straight at heaven, such as his "Undertake for me!" Remember, meditation's purpose is for the heart to be moved toward God by a clearer understanding. A clearer understanding of how desperately we need him and how we have nothing apart from his grace can also bear fruit as our hearts cry out to him. This too is meditation and communion with God.

Remember the Character of Your Redeemer

If we devote ourselves to regular, stated meditation, we can expect resistance from without and within. The world will entice us with its "thousand nothings of the hour" and "their stupefying power."[8] Our flesh will urge us to get "a little sleep, a little slumber, a little folding of the hands to rest" (Prov. 24:33). The devil will goad us to give up, ever throwing our failures in our faces. But remember that we serve a gracious God. When he sent his Son into the world, he sent him on a break-no-bruised-reeds

8. Matthew Arnold, "The Buried Life," 1852.

mission (Isa. 42:3). What Paul says about God's accepting our material gifts applies equally to his accepting our devoted gifts of meditation: "For if there is first a willing mind, it is accepted according to what one has, and not according to what he does not have" (2 Cor. 8:12).

As we press on and push through, always in conscious and constant dependence on God, he will escort us to the peak. And then, the View! *O altitudo!*

Reflection and Praxis

1. If finding time to pray and meditate is hard for you, consider the discipline of simplicity for the sake of communion with God. Review what you do with your discretionary time and ask the Spirit to show you how best to simplify your life so that you may deepen the intimacy of your friendship with Christ. Remember, as strange as it sounds and as hard as it is to believe, he wants to be with you (John 14:1–3; 17:3, 24).

2. Finding time is not our only challenge to meditation; we have distractions. Jozef Pieper suggests that perhaps "the greatest menace to our capacity for contemplation is the incessant fabrication of tawdry empty stimuli which kill the receptivity of the soul."[9] Again, take stock, asking yourself which of the world's many "tawdry empty stimuli" are crippling your ability to attend to our Lord. If you find some, how will you drive them away?

3. Our memory and imagination come first in meditation, because we need to have the object of our thoughts in mind.

9. Jozef Pieper, *Happiness and Contemplation* (South Bend, IN: St. Augustine's Press, 1979), 102.

The object of our thoughts is God as he reveals himself to us in creation and his Word. Therefore, a life devoted to meditation begins with devotion to knowing the Scriptures. There are many lectionaries and Bible-reading plans to choose from, or you can make your own. But if you don't have a plan, set one today. Ask God to give you the resolve to know his Word backward and forward before you leave this world.

4. Our understanding comes next in meditation, because we need to understand what God reveals about himself, so that our affections are guided by truth. That means we need to develop skills of interpretation. Some of those skills are the basic skills of reading that we all learn in school. Some are as simple as the *who-what-where-when-why-how* interrogation of the text we used in chapter 3. We can start with those and add other skills with discipline, study, and maturity. I will suggest some resources below.

5. Sometimes, especially when we know the Lord well, we are affected almost spontaneously by the truth of his Word. It's a habit of the heart that we can develop. Here's a simple exercise if this is new to you.

- First, pray.
  - Ask God to incline your heart to him in love (Ps. 119:36–37).
  - Ask him to give you his Spirit of wisdom and revelation to understand his word (Eph. 1:17).
  - Ask him to evoke and train your affections by his Word (1 Peter 1:8).
- Next, choose a brief text to read and reflect on. If you don't have anything in mind, choose one of these:
  - Genesis 1:1, 1:26–31, or 3:1–24

- Exodus 3:1–15
- Deuteronomy 6:1–9 (or the whole chapter)
- Psalms 23, 42, 121
- Matthew 4:1–11; 6:25–34
- Luke 15:1–7 or 19:41–44
- John 3:16–21, 8:12–30, 13:1–20, 14:1–14, 15:1–17, 17:1–26, 18:33–40, 19:16–37, or 20:11–18
- 2 Corinthians 4
- Ephesians 2

• Once you have a sense of the meaning of the text, determine which affections would be most appropriate in response. Make a note of the affection and what in the text evokes it.

Common Affections

Love	Sadness	Relief
Hatred	Hope	Anger
Desire	Gratitude	Despair
Aversion	Compassion	Fear
Joy/Delight	Zeal	Boldness

• Now compose a brief prayer either to express the biblical affection or to ask God to move your heart.
  - For example, suppose you read John 3:16–21. The text is packed with ideas, but you focus on the phrase from verse 18, "He who believes in Him is not condemned."
  - Because you believe in him, you have a fresh realization that you are not condemned. You imagine the loss and anguish of condemnation, and you feel a shiver of *fear* of what might have been, followed by a wave of *relief* and *gratitude*.
  - So you pray, "Holy Father, I hesitate to even express what my destiny would have been if you had not in your love

sent your Son to rescue me. My heart can only sigh in inexpressible relief. How I thank you for the indescribable gift of your Son!"

• Close with a prayer of thanksgiving to God for his holy Word and for creating us to know and love him.

Suggestions for Further Reading

Timothy Keller learned prayer, meditation, and communion with God from Augustine, John Owen, Jonathan Edwards, and other reliable guides; he restates and applies their teaching in *Prayer: Experiencing Awe and Intimacy with God* (New York: Dutton, 2014).

If you are getting started with understanding the Bible, try Douglas Stuart and Gordon D. Fee, *How to Read the Bible for All Its Worth*, 4th ed. (Grand Rapids: Zondervan, 2014) and R.C. Sproul, *Knowing Scripture*, expanded/3rd ed. (Downers Grove, IL: IVP Books, 2016). A more recent book, surprisingly deep for its brevity, is Jonathan Pennington, *Come and See: The Journey of Knowing God through Scripture* (Wheaton, IL: Crossway, 2023).

If you'd like to know more about the role of the affections in the Christian life, James K. A. Smith's *You Are What You Love: The Spiritual Power of Habit* (Grand Rapids: Brazos Press, 2016) is a recent application of Augustine's teaching on ordered love in the context of secular culture. The discussion of the affections has a long history, complicated by competing views of human psychology; Matthew A. Lapine details that complexity in *The Logic of the Body: Retrieving Theological Psychology* (Bellingham, WA: Lexham Press, 2020).

8

the devoted mind
seeks one thing

You want me to tell you why God is to be loved and how much. I answer, the reason for loving God is God Himself; and the measure of love due to Him is immeasurable love. Is this plain?

—BERNARD OF CLAIRVAUX

The One Thing

If theology is the study of God and all things in relation to God, we could say that the devoted mind is *theological*, for it contemplates God and all things in relation to God. God is its first and best thought. The devoted mind, born of God's Spirit, is God-flavored and looks at the world through God-colored glasses.

We could also say that the devoted mind is *theophilic*, for it loves God and all things in relation to God. That is, a heart made new by the Spirit, seeing God more and more clearly, knowing him more and more fully, inclines toward him more and more vigorously. The affections and longings of the believer should therefore be more and more God-leaning and God-centered.

Two models of this theophilic, one-thing mindset are King David and Mary of Bethany. David distills everything he wants from God into a single request:

> One thing I have desired of the LORD,
> That will I seek:
> That I may dwell in the house of the LORD
> All the days of my life,
> To behold the beauty of the LORD,
> And to inquire in His temple. (Ps. 27:4)

David's interest in the house of the Lord isn't the smell of the incense or the fine handwork of the woven curtains or the well-wrought almond blossoms of the golden lampstand, as fine as those things are. The object of his affections, the one thing that will satisfy him, is to see the beauty of the Lord. He is convinced that his happiness is inseparably bound to the contemplation of his Beloved and communion with him.

In Luke 10, Mary of Bethany finds her desire at the feet of Jesus:

> Now it happened as they went that [Jesus] entered a certain village; and a certain woman named Martha welcomed Him into her house. And she had a sister called Mary, who also sat at Jesus' feet and heard His word. But Martha was distracted with much serving, and she approached Him and said, "Lord, do You not care that my sister has left me to serve alone? Therefore tell her to help me."
>
> And Jesus answered and said to her, "Martha, Martha, you are worried and troubled about many things. But one thing is needed, and Mary has chosen that good part, which will not be taken away from her." (Luke 10:38–42)

Mary's affections glue her to her Master; she craves his words, his wisdom, his pleasure. This is her one thing—*he* is her one thing. Jesus seals her affections with his unqualified approval and declares that her fixed attention to him is the *one thing needed*.

Remember from the previous chapter that spiritual affections are motions deep inside us that are evoked by reflection on God and heavenly things. When our understanding judges something beautiful, our heart delights in it, as David delights in the beauty of the Lord and Mary delights in her beloved Jesus. At least, our heart delights in the beautiful when all is working as it should. But sin's corruption of our human nature has hobbled our thinking, distorted our affections, hardened our conscience, and weakened our resolve.

When we come to Christ by faith, he renews us by his Spirit. And the Spirit's work of sanctification is thorough; it doesn't stop with our thoughts but extends to our "whole spirit, soul, and body" (1 Thess. 5:23). Yes, our sanctification in this life is *partial* in one sense: although we will grow by the Spirit till our last breath, we won't reach full Christlikeness till we see him face to face (1 John 3:2). But our sanctification is *thorough* in that the Spirit renews every power of our souls that was corrupted by original sin.

My musician friend tells me that if you hold down the rightmost pedal on a piano so the strings are free to vibrate and then sing a note into the piano, you will hear one or more strings ring in sympathetic resonance with your voice. David and Mary show us the sympathetic resonance of renewed hearts: the Beloved sings, and when we draw close the strings of our hearts respond, tuned to his pitch by the Spirit. Think of John the Baptist, filled with the Spirit from his conception, leaping inside Elizabeth's womb when Mary came close, carrying the unborn Jesus (Luke 1:39–45). Spiritual affections are our hearts stretching, even leaping toward the *one thing* (Song 5:6).

But how? What do renewed affections look like, and how do we distinguish them from ordinary emotions? What marks the work of the Spirit on our longings and inclinations, our loves?

Unsurprisingly yet thrillingly, the marks of mature affections all center on God as he is revealed in and by Christ.

Love God for Himself

I say "unsurprisingly" because the First and Great Commandment is to love God with every power of our soul:

> "Teacher, which is the great commandment in the law?"
> Jesus said to him, "'You shall love the LORD your God with all your heart, with all your soul, and with all your mind.' This is the first and great commandment." (Matt. 22:36–38)

The better we get to know God, the more this command becomes our delight. We realize that he, and he alone, can be loved for himself alone. He is the only one who deserves to be loved to the depth and breadth and height our souls can reach. We love him for the perfections of his infinite, eternal, and unchangeable being, which bewilders us. We love him for his holiness. We love him for his inescapable presence. We love him for his unbounded and inexhaustible power and knowledge and wisdom. So with Ethan the Ezrahite, we ask, "Who in the heavens can be compared to the LORD? Who among the sons of the mighty can be likened to the LORD?" (Ps. 89:6).

And when we lift our eyes to gaze at God in his Father-Son-Spirit fullness as revealed in Christ, love spills over everywhere:

- God is love (1 John 4:8, 16; 2 Cor. 13:11).
- The Father loves the Son (John 3:35; 5:20; 10:17; 15:9; 17:23).

- The Father declares his love for his beloved Son (Matt. 3:17; 17:5; 2 Peter 1:17).
- The Son loves the Father (John 14:31).
- The Son abides in the Father's love (John 15:10).
- The Father loved us so much he sent his Son for us (John 3:16; 1 John 4:14).
- The Father loved us and the Son died for us while we were sinners (Rom. 5:8).
- The Father loved us enough to make us his children (1 John 3:1).
- The Son teaches us what love is by dying for us (1 John 3:16).
- The Son makes the Father known to us so that the Father's love for the Son will be in us (John 17:26).
- The Spirit has poured the love of God into our hearts (Rom. 5:5).
- The fruit of the Spirit is love (Gal. 5:22).

God is love indeed—wondrous love! And all this love is poured into us as God shares himself with us in Christ, unites us to him by his Spirit, and makes us in some mysterious way to partake in his divine nature (1 Peter 1:4). More than this, all the highest happiness and blessedness we can possibly know is to be had simply by the face-to-face vision of him we will have in Christ forever (Matt. 5:8; 1 Cor. 13:12).

This is the love-work of our minds and hearts: to contemplate God and not stop till our hearts go out to him in love. And that love opens our eyes and compels us to look more closely at him, and a closer look reveals more beauty, more loveliness, which in turn fires our affections toward him more vigorously still. I call this the *theophilic spiral*, and it spins on through eternity. "And through eternity, I'll sing on, I'll sing on!"[1]

1. "What Wondrous Love Is This," American folk hymn.

God himself is the first and highest object of our renewed affections.

Love All Things for God in Them

Another mark that our affections are renewed by the Spirit is that we love created things not for themselves alone but for God as we see him in them. No matter how good and beautiful some created thing is—whether a sunset across the Serengeti that takes our breath away or a friend so close she's almost a second self—if our affections for them don't reach beyond them to their source in God, our affections are not spiritual but earthly.

Recall the section "The Meaning of Everything in Three Prepositions" in chapter 6: all thing are *of* God, *through* God, and *to* God (Rom. 11:36); therefore our love for all things has its source in God and its strength in God and is ultimately for his glory. God alone is loved for himself, and all other things are loved for his sake. After all, anything in a creature that is true, noble, pure, lovely, virtuous, or praiseworthy has its source in God. And the more of God we find in something, the more we will love it. Even Christ.

Even Christ? Well, yes. In Jesus, the uncreated divine is uniquely united to the created human, in a way incomprehensible to us. The human nature is indivisible from the divine in him. He is the "express image" of "the invisible God" (Heb. 1:3; Col. 1:15) and "in Him dwells all the fullness of the Godhead bodily" (Col. 2:9). We love the man Christ Jesus above all creatures because God is in him "without measure" (John 3:34 ESV).

As we mature in Christ, we find that the more a created thing shows God's beauty or stirs our love for him or lifts our hearts to worship him, the more we will love it. Our favorite devotional literature, whether Augustine's *Confessions* or Owen's *The Glory of Christ* or any other, will be our favorite because it draws us closer to our Beloved. Eric Liddell—at least the film version of Eric Liddell—explained why he loved to run when he said, "God made me fast. And when I run, I feel His pleasure."[2] The closer we get to God, the more we see that every good thing in creation comes from him and leads us to thank and praise him (James 1:17). We learn even to see and appreciate our friends through Christ, and we will cherish most those friends who help us toward God.

Delight in Worship

David, that man after God's own heart (1 Sam. 13:14; Acts 13:22), has more to teach us about the *one thing*. He teaches us that those whose affections are renewed by the Spirit find a singular pleasure in gathered worship.

> How lovely is Your tabernacle,
> O LORD of hosts!
> My soul longs, yes, even faints
> For the courts of the LORD;
> My heart and my flesh cry out for the living God.
>
> Even the sparrow has found a home,
> And the swallow a nest for herself,
> Where she may lay her young—
> Even Your altars, O LORD of hosts,
> My King and my God.
> Blessed are those who dwell in Your house;
> They will still be praising You. *Selah* (Ps. 84:1–4)

2. *Chariots of Fire*, directed by Hugh Hudson (1981).

And the greater Son of David, our Lord Jesus Christ, often declared his delight in and zeal for divine worship. He followed the commands of God as given through Moses; he rebuked those who corrupted holy worship. The most striking example is his making a whip and driving the money changers out of the temple. When his disciples saw this, they applied David's words to him: "Zeal for Your house has eaten Me up" (John 2:17; see Ps. 69:9).

What makes corporate worship such a delight to us is that God is in it. God is present when his people gather as his living temple (1 Peter 2:5). In worship, God is present to give a greater sense of his love for us and to supply us with his strengthening, sanctifying grace. We come to worship to receive a growing sense of God's love in Jesus Christ. Without assurance of God's love for us in Christ, how will we have peace or joy or encouragement to take up our cross and follow Christ? How will we deny ourselves for the sake of his kingdom? But the Holy Spirit pours the love of God in our hearts (Rom. 5:5) and testifies in our hearts that we are God's beloved children (Rom. 8:15–16).

If we trace a typical flow of public worship, looking to see what God intends along the way, his love meets us everywhere:

- The *call to worship* is not from the pastor or from the church; it is from God, pronounced by the pastor from God's Word. God summons and welcomes us into his presence: "Welcome, my children! Come in!" He wants us to be with him, to behold his glory (John 17:24). He loves us.
- Our *corporate confession of sin* is our recognition that we are not worthy to cross his threshold. But he quickly responds to our confession to assure us of his pardon: "If we confess our sins, He is faithful and just to forgive

us our sins and to cleanse us from all unrighteousness"
(1 John 1:9). He loves us.

- We respond to his forgiveness in Christ with *doxology* and
  praise, lifting our voices to rejoice in him. He is enthroned
  on our praise; the Living Word dwells in our song (Ps.
  22:3; Col. 3:16).

- He speaks to us in *the readings from his Word* and *the
  preaching of his Word*, speaking to us as a Father to his child,
  shaping us, correcting us, building our hope, affirming his
  love (2 Tim. 3:16; Heb. 4:12). We hear our Beloved's voice,
  and our hearts leap up when he speaks (Song 5:6).

- We present our *tithes and offerings* to him, honoring him
  as the one who gave us all that we have (1 Chron. 29:14),
  and he receives our gifts as a fragrant offering (Phil. 4:18;
  Heb. 13:16).

- In our *prayers* we ask him for all that we need to serve and
  glorify him; we ask him to extend his kingdom through
  the world and bring light to the nations. We experience
  him as our heavenly Father who provides all we need. He
  hears us because he loves us (1 John 5:14).

- In *the Lord's Supper* he welcomes us as intimates at his
  table; we eat and drink his love, proclaiming his death,
  and in his death his love (1 Cor. 10:16; 11:26).

- The *benediction*, like the call to worship, is not from the
  pastor but from God. It comes from his Word and declares
  God's blessing on us, his assurance that even as we leave,
  his blessing follows us. He is our God and we are his
  people. He loves us.

If through the service of worship God announces his love to
us, pours his love into our hearts, and shares himself with us,
yet we are indifferent, cold, and distracted—such ingratitude is
unthinkable. His Spirit in us won't have it. Renewed hearts must

return love for love and exalt his name to the skies. Therefore our souls long, yes, even faint for the courts of the Lord (Ps. 84:2).

Caveat Amans *(Let the Lover Beware)*

Though the affections are powerful, not all are godly. Because of the remnants of sin in believers, we must guard our hearts. In "A Litany," John Donne acknowledges our danger and our need for God's protection when he prays "That our affections kill us not, nor die." We ask God to preserve our desire for him, that our love never die, but because of the dark side of desire, we ask God to stop our affections from killing us.

We often judge our experience in worship by how deeply we're moved. But the depth of a feeling says nothing about its object. Rut Etheridge confesses that when he's deeply moved in worship, it isn't necessarily toward God: "Maybe what I'm actually enthralled with is not so much God as the idea of my being enthralled with God. Maybe I'm worshiping my worship, or worshiping myself worshiping."[3]

So, as I said, we guard our hearts. But I need to add a caveat to our caveat. Becoming too self-conscious about our affections, always checking to see whether we're feeling deeply and whether our heart is vibrating to the Spirit's tune or to our flesh's, will paralyze us. It will kill the joy of loving God and all things in relation to God; it will dull the delight of worshiping our Beloved. It will turn us in on ourselves, away from the One Thing.

What then? When in doubt, pray. Donne's prayer is perfect, but his way with words might not fit you. Ask God to fill you with holy desires and longings for him and all things in relation

---

3. Rut Etheridge III, *God Breathed: Connecting through Scripture to God, Others, the Natural World, and Yourself* (Pittsburgh, PA: Crown & Covenant Publications, 2019), 36.

to him and to deliver you "from all disordered and sinful affections."[4] Ask the Spirit to show you when your affections spring from the wrong fountain. And above all, enjoy your Beloved!

Reflection and Praxis

1. As Bernard of Clairvaux says, "The reason for loving God is God Himself." Write a prayer to God telling him not only that you love him but why. Be specific. Tell him what he is to you. Tell him what you find lovely in him. As you write, rejoice in him "with joy inexpressible and full of glory" (1 Peter 1:8).

2. John Owen says that one mark of earthly or unrenewed affections (affections that outwardly appear to be for God but are not) is that they are fleeting; we might feel them often, but they never settle in to stay. Can you think of some ways to watch for them without becoming overly self-conscious?

3. What are some things in corporate worship that might stir feelings that are deep and enjoyable, yet not godly? For one example, look at Ezekiel 33:30–33. Can you think of other examples in the Bible?

4. We are more certain to taste God's love in Christ that we are offered in worship if we prepare our hearts and draw near to God full of desire and expectation that he will draw near to us (James 4:8). What are some specific ways you can prepare your heart to receive God's love in worship? William S. Plumer's exhortation about worship might suggest some ideas: "In all acts of worship let us summon our whole nature to the work; let our intellects

---

4. From "The Great Litany" in *The Book of Common Prayer* (Huntington Beach, CA: Anglican Liturgy Press, 2019), 92.

know God, our wills choose him, our hearts go out after him, our confidence lean on him, our love delight in him, our tongues praise him, and our hands clap for joy of him."[5]

5. One reason we delight in corporate worship is that in the service God's love for us is displayed, reaffirmed, communicated, and tasted. Another reason is that in worship we honor our Beloved and "Give unto the LORD the glory due to His name" (Ps. 29:2). What relationship do you see between his declaring his love for us and our giving him glory?

6. If you are in some way responsible for worship services in your church, what are some ways you can cultivate a hunger in the congregation to taste God's love when you worship?

Suggestions for Further Reading

If you haven't yet read Augustine's *Confessions*, now is the time.

---

5. William S. Plumer, *Psalms: A Critical and Expository Commentary with Doctrinal and Practical Remarks* (Edinburgh: The Banner of Truth Trust, 1975), 917.

9

the devoted mind rejects God's rival

If all those glittering Monarchs, that command
The servile quarters of this earthly ball,
Should tender in exchange their shares of land,
I would not change my fortunes for them all:
Their wealth is but a counter to my coin:
The world's but theirs; but my Belovèd's mine.
—Francis Quarles

Jane Austen's chief end in *Pride and Prejudice* is to marry Miss Elizabeth Bennet to Mr. Darcy, that "single man in possession of a good fortune." One of the several obstacles to that end is George Wickham, dashing in uniform, distinguished in speech, yet dishonorable in ways hidden from Miss Bennet. Her heart is almost captured by his charm, till Mr. Darcy reveals Wickham's history and character to her in a letter.[1] This unmasking untangles Elizabeth's affections from Wickham, clearing the way for Mr. Darcy to win her.

---

1. The letter is in chapter 35 of *Pride and Prejudice*.

Two competing for the heart of one is a common theme in literature and life. The struggle can be comic or tragic, lighthearted or vicious. And strange as it sounds, our hearts are the object of the love triangle of most consequence.

Strange, indeed. Owen catches its irony and implausibility: "The great contest of heaven and earth is about the affections of the poor worm which we call man."[2] It isn't news that the world has designs on us; we can't avoid its advances. But the Holy One, the Maker of heaven and earth, the Ruler of all, the Lord of glory, the one who is "most high above all the earth" and "exalted far above all gods" (Ps. 97:9)—why should he condescend to contend for our affections? What can that even mean? George Herbert was justly baffled by God's interest in us:

> My God, what is a heart,
> That thou shouldst it so eye, and woo,
> Pouring upon it all thy art,
> As if that thou hadst nothing else to do?[3]

Lock, Stock, and Barrel

God wants all of you. He says, "My son, give me your heart" (Prov. 23:26), and your heart is you, all of you. Your heart is so precious to God that he'll accept nothing from you unless your affections come with it. Pile up your costliest treasures to sacrifice, but if your heart isn't on the altar, God will have none of it: "And now, Israel, what does the LORD your God require of you, but to fear the LORD your God, to walk in all His ways and to love

2. John Owen, *The Grace and Duty of Being Spiritually Minded*, 1681, reprinted in *The Works of John Owen*, ed. William H. Goold, 24 vols. (Edinburgh: Johnstone & Hunter, 1850–1855; reprint by Banner of Truth Trust, 1965, 1991), 7:395.

3. Herbert, "Matins," lines 9–12.

Him, to serve the Lord your God *with all your heart and with all your soul*" (Deut. 10:12). That's a tall order.

But God, being the kind of God he is, designs his grace to rework our hearts so that we *can* give ourselves to him: "The Lord your God will circumcise your heart and the heart of your descendants, to love the Lord your God with all your heart and with all your soul, that you may live" (Deut. 30:6). These hopeful words become the cherished core of the new covenant that God makes with us in Christ:

> Behold, the days are coming, says the Lord, when I will make a new covenant with the house of Israel and with the house of Judah—not according to the covenant that I made with their fathers in the day that I took them by the hand to lead them out of the land of Egypt, My covenant which they broke, though I was a husband to them, says the Lord. But this is the covenant that I will make with the house of Israel after those days, says the Lord: I will put My law in their minds, and write it on their hearts; and I will be their God, and they shall be My people. No more shall every man teach his neighbor, and every man his brother, saying, "Know the Lord," for they all shall know Me, from the least of them to the greatest of them, says the Lord. For I will forgive their iniquity, and their sin I will remember no more. (Jer. 31:31–34)[4]

But God is not the only one out for our hearts. The world, God's archrival for our affections, presses its suit for the same prize. God as our Maker has a legitimate claim on us; the world,

---

4. See also Ezekiel 36:26–27 and Hebrews 8:7–13. For a helpful discussion of the newness of the New Covenant, see Michael Allen, *Sanctification* (New Studies in Dogmatics; Grand Rapids: Zondervan Academic, 2017), 177–83.

however, would steal our hearts. It makes its lying promises, and it wines and dines us to catch and keep our affections. And those who are taken in and prefer the world to God are rejected by the one they have rejected (Prov. 1:24–31). Jesus marvels at such a choice: "For what profit is it to a man if he gains the whole world, and is himself destroyed or lost?" (Luke 9:25).

Yes, it's hard to believe. But our hearts are the object of the love triangle of most consequence—eternal consequence.

How Did We Get to Be So Popular?

Why such interest in our hearts? Well, suppose a friend gives you a framed print of Vincent van Gogh's *Café Terrace at Night*. How precious is her gift? Before you answer, suppose she waits tables at a diner and worked double shifts for two months to save for the print. How precious would you say? But what if, instead, she didn't really want to give it to you at all and told you to your face she intended it for her cousin and only gave it to you because her mother made her? What has she given you but contempt?

Whether she gives you a used tea bag or an original van Gogh, her gift will be more (or less) precious to you depending on how much (or little) of her heart comes with it. When we give our affections, we give all we have. To give our hearts is to give ourselves away. Therefore, when we keep God's commands or suffer for his name's sake, if our keeping or suffering doesn't flow from a heart cemented to him in love, he despises it. Speaking through Isaiah, he says,

> Inasmuch as these people draw near with their mouths
> And honor Me with their lips,
> But have removed their hearts far from Me,
> And their fear toward Me is taught by the command-
> ment of men,

> Therefore, behold, I will again do a marvelous work
> Among this people,
> A marvelous work and a wonder;
> For the wisdom of their wise men shall perish,
> And the understanding of their prudent men shall be
> hidden. (Isa. 29:13–14)

This, by the way, explains how we can be immersed in this world day in and day out, working hard at our jobs and making wise investments and cultivating an appreciation for van Gogh, yet not be enslaved to the world. If we don't give our affections to the world, whatever we give—our work, our trade, our time, even our interest—we don't give ourselves. That detachment keeps us from a disordered love for the world. That detachment makes all the difference.[5]

The Beloved Unmasks His Rival

Miss Elizabeth Bennet is saved from a ruined life when Mr. Darcy exposes George Wickham for what he is. Still, *Pride and Prejudice* doesn't end well for everyone. Elizabeth's sister Lydia lacks a clearheaded perspective on Wickham and so falls for him. Their life together is burdened by too little money, too much spending, and frequent moves "from place to place in quest of a cheap situation." Predictably, Wickham's affection for Lydia soon sinks into "indifference."[6]

Infinitely more tragic is the lot of the countless unbelievers who, lacking a clearheaded perspective on the world, succumb to its seduction. They believe its promise that if you give it your heart, all your wildest dreams will come true and the things you

---

5. See also the previous chapter about loving all things in relation to God.
6. Austen, *Pride and Prejudice*, chapter 61.

most fear will not. We're tempted to shake our heads at their gullibility, but apart from God's grace, we are all dupes for the lies of the world.

In God's grace, he unmasks the vanity of the world and its demonic designs on our hearts. If we ignore his kind warnings, we show contempt for our Beloved's wisdom and goodness. Therefore, it is the loving labor of the devoted mind to attend carefully to God's unmasking of his rival.

God Unmasks the World by the Life and Cross of Christ

If there were any truth to the world's claims, if its crowns and empires were as precious as they promise, do you think the Father would have kept them from his Son? Yet Christ walked this world with no place to lay his head and with never more than the daily bread he told us to pray for. When the time came for him to leave the world, he was nailed naked to a cross of shame. In that cross, the world boasted of its power and bared its own shameless face.

With his renewed and devoted mind, Paul took one look at the cross and said that by it "the world has been crucified to me, and I to the world" (Gal. 6:14)—as if he said, "Since I have believed in Christ and tasted the power of his cross, I'm done with the world. I'll take none of its trinkets and give it none of my heart."

How can we live under the cross and practice such unworldly detachment? We can't run to the desert to escape the siren call of the world. Paul himself tells us to work hard in the world, to make sure we have something to share with those in need (Eph. 4:28). We can't "shine as lights in the world" (Phil. 2:15) unless we live surrounded by its darkness. This life we're called to—working and engaging with the world, yet not loving the world—is risky business.

Sometimes it's hard to know whether we're being faithful or giving our hearts away. More on that in a moment. But in the face of the world's flirting, we must keep our eyes on Jesus. Look at how he comes to us in the gospel: despised, scorned, hounded, and pierced—all by this world. How could we give ourselves to the one who nailed our Beloved to the tree? Shouldn't we rather say with Ignatius, "My love is crucified, and there is no fire in me for another love"?[7]

God Unmasks the World in the Lives of His Apostles

Christ gave us the apostles not only to teach us his Word but to model his way of life, so they walked the road he walked. God did great work through them. Through them he laid the foundation of his church throughout the world. To facilitate their work he could have given them positions of honor or power in the world, made them princes or bishops or bankers, so that they could win a hearing with governors and kings. But his infinite wisdom instead led their way through hardships; they lived and died in poverty, distress, persecution, and reproach. God made them models not of the world's greatness but of light, grace, zeal, and holiness. As he had done with his Son, God showed in the apostles how little we need in this world in order to taste his love and favor.

> I think that God has displayed us, the apostles, last, as men condemned to death; for we have been made a spectacle to the world, both to angels and to men. We are fools for Christ's sake, but you are wise in Christ! We are weak, but you are strong! You are distinguished, but we are dishonored! To the present hour we both hunger and thirst, and we are poorly clothed, and beaten, and homeless. And we labor,

7. Ignatius of Antioch, "The Third Epistle of the Same St. Ignatius [to the Ephesians]," in *The Apostolic Fathers with Justin Martyr and Irenaeus*, ed. Alexander Roberts, James Donaldson, and A. Cleveland Coxe, vol. 1, *The Ante-Nicene Fathers* (Buffalo: Christian Literature Co., 1885), 104.

working with our own hands. Being reviled, we bless; being persecuted, we endure; being defamed, we entreat. We have been made as the filth of the world, the offscouring of all things until now. (1 Cor. 4:9–13)

God held these men dear, as his best friends. Why then would we think that we need the pleasures of this world to serve him faithfully and drink his love?

God Unmasks the World by Giving It to His Enemies

Who was the wickedest person in history, the vilest enemy of God and mankind? The twentieth century is crowded with candidates, from Hitler to Stalin to Idi Amin. Then there are Nero and Genghis Khan and the lesser-known Vlad the Impaler, who lived down to his name. We need not enumerate their cruelties. We know the world groaned beneath their savagery. Yet God in his providence gave them each dazzling wealth and the pleasures that this world has to offer.

That should tell us something. If land and gold and palaces and fame and power and indulgence had real, lasting value in themselves, would our holy and wise God lavish them on those who most hate him and his people? Should we set our affections on the things that God pours into the lascivious laps of the wicked, things that become a snare to them and pile up wrath against them for the day of judgment? What can those who truly love God do when they think of this but turn their backs on the world and seek true treasure in the spiritual and eternal, in Christ?

God Unmasks the World in Its Failure to Make Good Its Promises

It's Christmas morning. You've just finished unwrapping your last present. On the floor at your feet (or parked in the driveway) is everything on your list, everything you wanted, everything you thought would make you happy. What, then, is this empty feeling?

If you are lucky enough to feel that emptiness, you are tasting the blessing that Solomon learned by experiment:

> Whatever my eyes desired I did not keep from them.
> I did not withhold my heart from any pleasure. . . .
> . . . .
> Then I looked on all the works that my hands had done
> And on the labor in which I had toiled;
> And indeed all was vanity and grasping for the wind.
> There was no profit under the sun. (Eccl. 2:10–11)

It's natural to assume that more is better. Nothing seems more obvious than that having more relieves the mind. But God in his mercy never lets the world bring us the ease and security and rest it promises. If only we let that emptiness teach us. Then "from the best bliss that earth imparts, we turn unfilled to thee again."[8]

God Warns Us of the Risk of Loving the World

God couldn't be plainer or more urgent in his drumbeat of warnings throughout Scripture. He's left no wiggle room of ambiguity. He completely unmasks the fangs of the world, and we know that entangling our affections in the world endangers our souls.

The love of money is a bright red flag:

> Those who desire to be rich fall into temptation and a snare,
> and into many foolish and harmful lusts which drown men
> in destruction and perdition. For the love of money is a root

---

8. Bernard of Clairvaux, "Jesus, Thou Joy of Loving Hearts," trans. Ray Palmer, 1858.

of all kinds of evil, for which some have strayed from the faith in their greediness, and pierced themselves through with many sorrows. (1 Tim. 6:9–10)

Jesus is unambiguous when he says that not one of us "can serve two masters; for either he will hate the one and love the other, or else he will be loyal to the one and despise the other. You cannot serve God and mammon" (Matt. 6:24). John is just as clear as his Master: "Do not love the world or the things in the world. If anyone loves the world, the love of the Father is not in him" (1 John 2:15).

Yet somehow many of us think ourselves immune to the commonest temptations.

A Way of Escape

It is God's grace to unmask his rival for us; it is our duty to take heed.[9] God put us in this world to live and work in it, and we have godly ways to get and spend, holy ways to enjoy his goodness in creation. What makes godly work and holy pleasure differ from giving your heart away to the world isn't always obvious. Telling the difference demands spiritual maturity and wisdom. But knowing the difference makes all the difference.

The film *Free Solo* documents Alex Honnold's successful quest to become the first person to climb El Capitan with just his body—no ropes, no safety gear, and no normal amygdala.[10] Amygdalae are almond-shaped structures in our brains that, when we sense danger, trigger fear and a fight-or-flight response. MRI studies of Honnold's brain, however, showed that his amygdalae were unaffected by the shocking images the

9. Remember, grace and duty are friends.
10. *Free Solo*, directed by Elizabeth Chai Vasarhelyi and Jimmy Chin (2018).

researcher showed him. It's likely that he was able to push himself to attempt something as bold as scaling El Capitan because he was incapable of ordinary fear.

Honnold's success notwithstanding, ordinary fear is a good thing, even more for our souls than for our bodies (Matt. 10:28). God's unmasking of the world should shock our spiritual amygdalae into high alert and prompt our flight from danger. A devoted mind will give the world a wide berth and not risk entangled affections.

Cultivating a fear of entanglement with the world is a necessary discipline of the spiritual mind because we naively underestimate the force of the world's attraction and just as naively overestimate our ability to pry ourselves free from its grip. How so? We naturally don't want to be thought priggish, so we keep step with those around us in the way we consume pop (or high) culture, or the way we spend time and wealth, or even the way we conduct friendships. If our consciences squirm, we of course acknowledge that Scripture condemns inordinate love of the world, but we rationalize our indulgence: *Our circumstances aren't like those in first-century Palestine. And don't forget the goodness of God's creation.*

True, our world is in many ways different from the world Paul lived in, and God's creation is good and he means us to enjoy it. That's why discerning risky from safe involvement in the world isn't easy. Paul shows us a safer path: "All things are lawful for me, but all things are not helpful. All things are lawful for me, but I will not be brought under the power of any" (1 Cor. 6:12).

Our Beloved has unmasked the cunning of the world and the weakness of our flesh. Unwilling to be drawn away from Jesus, let's seek from him the grace that enabled Paul to say, "I discipline my body and bring it into subjection, lest, when I have preached to others, I myself should become disqualified" (1 Cor. 9:27).

Reflection and Praxis

1. Describe, as specifically as you can, why it's surprising that God seeks *your* heart, *your* love. Why does God want your heart? How can his desire for your affections motivate your self-denial?

2. How is it that we can be diligent and industrious in our duties in the world, engaged with the culture, yet not be entangled in inordinate love for the world? Do you know someone who models this? If so, describe that person.

3. When we think of spiritual disciplines, we often have in mind solo efforts, such as our private prayer, meditation on the Scriptures, fasting, simplicity, and habit formation. But Christ calls us into his body, and Paul constantly reminds us of our corporate life in Christ. What are some ways believers can help to guard one another from worldly entanglement without becoming the pleasure police?

Suggestions for Further Reading

For a biblical and theological foundation for self-denial, see Michael Allen's chapters "Heavenly-Mindedness" and "Self-Denial" in *Grounded in Heaven: Recentering Christian Hope and Life on God* (Grand Rapids: Eerdmans, 2018), 89–158. I especially appreciate his focus on self-denial for the sake of communion with our Lord.

10

the devoted mind
seeks and is changed

*And the soul is moved by heavenly love and longing when,
having clearly beheld the beauty and the fairness of the
Word of God, it falls deeply in love with His loveliness.*
—Origen

The Copyist and the Lover

In John Sloan's 1908 etching *Copyist at the Metropolitan Museum*, a dozen men, women, and children crowd around a painter who has arranged her easel, canvas, and palette in front of a work she's copying. The original on the wall before her depicts a shepherd and his flock. My interest is in the copyist herself—her position, posture, and gaze. She leans forward from the hip, her nose within a foot of the shepherd, her brush ready in hand. We see her face in profile, her eyes wide in observation. She is oblivious to the crowd. Her unbroken gaze is that of a student, poring over brush strokes and lighting and shading and composition and color, reverse-engineering the master's technique so she can create a faithful copy.

Like Sloan's copyist, we believers glue our wide eyes to a Shepherd. We attend to details, block out distractions, and again and again refer to the Original. But our goal is a faithful copy of a *life*: the life of the one who is life. And our gaze is that of a student but more than a student's: ours is the gaze of a lover. So when Paul reminds us of our calling as copyists, he doesn't teach us a technique; he leads us in worship:

> Let this mind be in you which was also in Christ Jesus, who, being in the form of God, did not consider it robbery to be equal with God, but made Himself of no reputation, taking the form of a bondservant, and coming in the likeness of men. And being found in appearance as a man, He humbled Himself and became obedient to the point of death, even the death of the cross. Therefore God also has highly exalted Him and given Him the name which is above every name, that at the name of Jesus every knee should bow, of those in heaven, and of those on earth, and of those under the earth, and that every tongue should confess that Jesus Christ is Lord, to the glory of God the Father. (Phil. 2:5–11)

Paul knows that God's purpose is that we be like Christ: "For whom He foreknew, He also predestined to be conformed to the image of His Son, that He might be the firstborn among many brethren" (Rom. 8:29). He knows that God created us as images and as imitators, who become like what we worship—whether we worship Christ or false gods:

> Their idols are silver and gold,
> The work of men's hands.
> They have mouths, but they do not speak;
> Eyes they have, but they do not see;
> They have ears, but they do not hear;

Noses they have, but they do not smell;
They have hands, but they do not handle;
Feet they have, but they do not walk;
Nor do they mutter through their throat.
Those who make them are like them;
So is everyone who trusts in them. (Ps. 115:4–8)

Because we are copyists who become like what we worship, the work of the Spirit in us to make us like Christ begins with our adoring contemplation, our noses a foot from the Shepherd, hearts wide open to take in every glorious detail of our Master. This is the spiritual mindedness of Romans 8:6, the devoted mind we're after. As Paul puts it in 2 Corinthians, "And we all, with unveiled face, beholding the glory of the Lord, are being transformed into the same image from one degree of glory to another. For this comes from the Lord who is the Spirit" (2 Cor. 3:18 ESV). Our attentive worship, as we gather with God's people on Sunday and daily commune with God in our devotions, is the primary way we "put on the new self, which is being renewed in knowledge after the image of its creator" (Col. 3:10 ESV). And, in the end, we will be made like Christ, once again through our loving gaze: "Beloved, now we are children of God; and it has not yet been revealed what we shall be, but we know that when He is revealed, we shall be like Him, for we shall see Him as He is" (1 John 3:2).

That's why not only our thoughts but also our affections are central to our sanctification. Whatever our affections cling to, whether the world or Christ, stamps its image on us like a seal pressed into warm wax. So we understand John's urgency when he pleads with us not to "love the world or the things in the world" (1 John 2:15) and to "keep [ourselves] from idols" (1 John 5:21). Jesus boiled it down for us: "Where your treasure is, there your heart will be also" (Matt. 6:21).

We met these ideas in chapter 5, where our focus was on our contemplation of Christ and communion with him. Now we turn to the powerful work of the Spirit through that contemplation, his power that inclines our hearts increasingly toward our Beloved in our gradual renewal (2 Cor. 4:16). As we fix our eyes on Jesus, our love grows more sincere, our delight more gratifying, our desire more urgent, and we are refreshed by our sight of him. Our minds become the temple of God where he dwells by his Spirit. Christ also dwells in us, and we in him: "God is love, and he who abides in love abides in God, and God in him" (1 John 4:16). This mutual indwelling is eternal life on earth; we know him and are known by him (John 17:3; 1 Cor. 13:12).

This mutual indwelling in love bears fruit as our lives are conformed to Christ's: "He who says he abides in Him ought himself also to walk just as He walked" (1 John 2:6). As Jesus put it in the upper room, "If you love me, you will keep my commandments" (John 14:15 ESV). That is, our love for Christ and all the godly affections that flow from our love animate our resolve to respond to our Beloved's beauty and love. We beg to know, *How can I please you, Lord?* (Eph. 5:10).

So, though our godly affections are pleasing in themselves to God and to us, they serve a further purpose. They are the bridge between our devoted thoughts of Christ and holy living. Think of the copyist. If she simply stood and admired the masterpiece, she would draw great pleasure from it, but her contemplation and admiration bear fruit in her own painting—a painting as like the masterpiece as her highest skills allow.

Good-Enough Love?

Because this increase of love that conforms us to Christ's image is gradual, Paul describes our growth in increments: "tribulation produces perseverance; and perseverance, character;

and character, hope" (Rom. 5:3–4). Peter says that by God's power we build Christlike lives like bricklayers, adding one grace to another:

> Giving all diligence, add to your faith virtue, to virtue knowledge, to knowledge self-control, to self-control perseverance, to perseverance godliness, to godliness brotherly kindness, and to brotherly kindness love" (2 Peter 1:5–7)

This takes time. It often feels like it's taking too much time; it's hard to see that we're any more like him than we were a year ago.

And sometimes our growth is immeasurably slow not because the Spirit's work in us is gradual and our expectations are high but because we settle for "good-enough love." Good-enough love, of course, isn't. Good-enough love forfeits all hope of Christlikeness. Good-enough love says, "I believe in Christ and am therefore God's child. He will never leave me or forsake me. My inheritance in heaven is sure and won't be any surer because I try harder. Of course I'll stay away from the Big Sins and go to church. That's enough. I'm no zealot." Good-enough love doesn't give its highest skill in "all diligence," isn't concerned to thrive in Christ, won't take trouble if trouble is needed to be transformed "from one degree of glory to another."

Paul says, "I do not count myself to have apprehended; but one thing I do, forgetting those things which are behind and reaching forward to those things which are ahead, I press toward the goal for the prize of the upward call of God in Christ Jesus" (Phil. 3:13–14), but good-enough love says, "I've apprehended; I'm depending on what lies behind; I'll wait for my prize." Good-enough love feels safe. The elders won't rebuke someone who shows up on Sunday and stays out of big trouble. And there are plenty of good-enough lovers around to reinforce each other in their passive discipleship.

But we all know what happens to a soul satisfied with half measures. Joy is impossible. Decay is inevitable. Christ is dishonored as unworthy. The gospel, which promises new life, is mocked. True peace of conscience is beyond reach.

How, when Jesus loved us to the end (John 13:1), can we settle for good-enough love? Rather, "let us go on to perfection. ... And this we will do if God permits" (Heb. 6:1, 3).

The Glory of Christ's Affections

The perfection we go on to includes conforming our affections to the pattern of Christ Jesus himself.[1] Christ's affections are glorious and display the zenith of love for God and neighbor (Matt. 22:37–40). In him we see unfallen human affections at work in a fallen world, and he calls us to follow his lead (John 13:34).

John 14:31 is the only place in the Gospels that says in so many words that Jesus loves the Father. But his love for God motivates everything he does for our salvation. When Jesus says, "My food is to do the will of Him who sent Me, and to finish His work" (John 4:34), he fulfills the words of David, "I delight to do Your will, O my God" (Ps. 40:8). The writer to the Hebrews gives us a cosmic glimpse of Christ's coming into the world to bring salvation with those very words from Psalm 40 on his lips:

Therefore, when He came into the world, He said:

> "Sacrifice and offering You did not desire,
> But a body You have prepared for Me.
> In burnt offerings and sacrifices for sin

---

1. For a detailed study of Christ's affections, see B. B. Warfield, "On the Emotional Life of our Lord," first published in *Biblical and Theological Studies by the Members of the Faculty of Princeton Theological Seminary* (New York: Charles Scribner's Sons, 1912), 35–90.

You had no pleasure.
Then I said, 'Behold, I have come—
In the volume of the book it is written of Me—
To do Your will, O God.'" (Heb. 10:5–7)

And see the uncompromising determination of his love: "Now it came to pass, when the time had come for Him to be received up, that He steadfastly set His face to go to Jerusalem," knowing it meant humiliation, suffering, and death on the cross (Luke 9:51). And as he knelt on the verge of enduring the full weight of it all, he remained submitted to the Father's will (Matt. 26:39).

As we trace his life through the Gospels with the eyes of our faith on him, we see the glory of his love for the Father—the full, unhesitating, holy inclination of his heart toward him—and the pattern of his love is impressed on us (2 Cor. 3:18).

Christ's affections are also prominent in his interactions with people. He sees their distress, their danger, their grief, their ignorance, their misery, and his heart is moved to pity. He has compassion on the weary and shepherdless multitudes (Matt. 9:35–38), compassion on the sick (Matt. 14:14), compassion on the hungry (Matt. 15:32), compassion on the blind (Matt. 20:34), compassion on the unclean (Mark 1:40–41), compassion on the demon-possessed (Mark 5:18–19), compassion on a grieving mother (Luke 7:12–14). Jesus weeps with those who weep (John 11:33–36). He sighs deeply in his spirit at those who refuse to see (Mark 8:11–12). He's even irritated when his disciples try to keep parents from bringing their children to him (Mark 10:13–16). Christ's affections embrace the full spectrum of the human heart.

What Love Is Good Enough?

The only love for God that is good enough is the love that Christ showed, the fullest fulfilling of the Great Commandment.

He loved God with his affections stretched to their highest reach, with all his heart, with all his soul, and with all his mind (Matt. 22:37). Our love to God is good enough, then, when it flows from Christ in us: when we prefer and value God above all things in every situation; when we cling to him and refuse to be separated from him regardless of the difficulties of life; when we do nothing at any time that isn't motivated and directed by love for him. This is what the greatness and perfection and beauty of God's nature requires; it is the only fitting answer to his love for us in Christ: "Love so amazing, so divine demands my soul, my life, my all."[2]

As we know, the Scriptures make clear that none of us attains to that perfection of love in this life. Even Paul, our preeminent example of Christlikeness, confessed his shortcoming even as he pledged his increasing love: "Not that I have already attained, or am already perfected; but I press on, that I may lay hold of that for which Christ Jesus has also laid hold of me" (Phil. 3:12). He knew he hadn't reached perfection; but he also saw God's grace at work in his life and bearing fruit through his striving by the Spirit: "But by the grace of God I am what I am, and His grace toward me was not in vain; but I labored more abundantly than they all, yet not I, but the grace of God which was with me" (1 Cor. 15:10).

At the end of his life, as he was awaiting his execution, he was able to say,

> The time of my departure is at hand. I have fought the good fight, I have finished the race, I have kept the faith. Finally, there is laid up for me the crown of righteousness, which the Lord, the righteous Judge, will give to me on that Day, and not to me only but also to all who have loved His appearing. (2 Tim. 4:6–8)

2. Isaac Watts, "When I Survey the Wondrous Cross," 1707.

When God's grace is at work in us and we, like Paul, are pressing on to Christlikeness, our affections will be marked by a readiness for spiritual things and a relish in spiritual things: a readiness and relish that pleases God.

Our Affections Will Be Ready for Spiritual Things

As we've seen, our minds are confronted by spiritual things in countless ways, from hard providence and temptation to corporate worship to our private meditations on Christ in his Word. In fact, everything in life and creation confronts us with God. When our affections are increasingly like Christ's, we welcome and embrace thoughts of him and run with them as far as our duties in life allow.

But we should be concerned when we put them off—when, for example, we're satisfied to show up to worship, sing, bow our heads, and present our offerings while our hearts are far from God. Or when we fill our time with diversions to crowd out Christ. Or when temptations work on us and we let them work, letting unjust anger or illicit desire simmer in our hearts rather than calling on Christ to drive the tempter away.

Our Affections Will Relish Spiritual Things

Christlike affections taste the goodness and graciousness of God in spiritual things (Ps. 34:8; 1 Peter 2:3). To taste God's goodness is to experience a savory relish and sweetness in communion with him. Sometimes that taste of God in Christ is almost too much for the soul to bear, and we rejoice in him "with joy inexpressible and full of glory" (1 Peter 1:8), yet that overwhelming taste of him never sates us so that we turn away like a "satisfied soul [that] loathes the honeycomb" (Prov. 27:7). On the contrary, our hunger for God is the best sauce, and thoughts of him are sweet to us even when they come wrapped in the bitter herbs of hard providence or the cross of self-denial: "To a hungry soul every bitter thing is sweet" (Prov. 27:7).

But we should be concerned when our affections are so filled with earthly things or even the base pleasures of sin that thoughts of God and heavenly things are like unsalted egg whites to us. When we lose our sense of taste for God in things, we couldn't be less like Christ.

When we are concerned about the health of our affections, and therefore of our inclination toward and love for God in Christ, we can remember the work of the copyist. She looks at the original, then at her work, then back at the original. If she's got the color off, or the figures are out of proportion, or the perspective is askew, she takes out her knife and scrapes off the canvas everything that strayed from the original. She studies the original and starts again. We likewise look to Christ and compare our lives to his to see where we've missed the mark. We pull out the knife of the Word of God, which is "sharper than any two-edged sword . . . and is a discerner of the thoughts and intents of the heart" (Heb. 4:12). By God's grace, we confess our sins and seek his Spirit's help to start again. We ask him to renew our affections after the image of Love incarnate, Jesus Christ.

Reflection and Praxis

1. Set aside several weeks to read through one of the Gospels. As you read, note every time you see Jesus moved by some affection, whether the text mentions it explicitly or you can infer it. Also note what comes of his affections: what he does or says. What patterns do you see?

2. The apostles call us not only to imitate Christ but to imitate others who imitate Christ. Paul says, "Imitate me, just as I also imitate Christ" (1 Cor. 11:1). He calls the Philippians to "join in following my example, and note those who so walk, as you have us for a pattern" (Phil. 3:17). In Hebrews, we're told to

"remember your leaders, those who spoke to you the word of God. Consider the outcome of their way of life, and imitate their faith" (13:7 ESV). Who do you know who displays Christ's love for God and others? What about the way they love reminds you of Christ and points you to him? How might you imitate them?

3. Ask the Spirit to search your heart to show you how ready your affections are for thoughts of God in Christ or of heavenly things. Ask him to show you where you are crowding Christ out of your thoughts and whether you've grown cold toward him. If he reveals that you have a reticence for spiritual things, confess your sins and receive God's forgiveness in Christ.

4. Ask the Spirit to search your heart to show you whether your affections relish and savor thoughts of God in Christ or of heavenly things. Ask him to show you where you have developed a taste for things that lead your heart away from Christ. If he reveals that you have a distaste for spiritual things, confess your sins and receive God's forgiveness in Christ.

Suggestions for Further Reading

Jason B. Hood's *Imitating God in Christ: Recapturing a Biblical Pattern* (Downers Grove, IL: IVP Academic, 2013) explores and recovers the biblical call to imitate Christ. B. B. Warfield's insightful 1912 essay on Christ's emotions, cited earlier in this chapter, has been reprinted in book form in the Crossway Short Classics Series: B. B. Warfield, *The Emotional Life of Our Lord* (Wheaton, IL: Crossway, 2022).

11

the devoted mind
finds life worth living

To be spiritually minded is life and peace.
—ROMANS 8:6

*I have come that they may have life, and that they may
have it more abundantly.*
—JOHN 10:10

*Peace I leave with you, My peace I give to you; not as the
world gives do I give to you.*
—JOHN 14:27

Dinner Is Served

When Paula announces from the kitchen, "Dinner's ready,"
the context of our relationship packs into those few words more
meaning than the simple status of the evening meal. She's invit-
ing (even summoning) me: "Come to the table." She's dangling
a multilayered incentive before my nose: "If you come, you shall
be nourished, delighted, and satisfied with food—and you shall

enjoy my company." She's also hinting at less savory consequences: "If you don't come now, your food will get cold" or (more personally) "my work will be ruined." And because she's my wife and not a short-order cook, much is at stake: "Come to the table and honor me with your love, or stay where you are and scorn me with ingratitude."

I put down my book and hurry to the table.

We often use shorthand to say much with few words. When the Pharisees try to trap Jesus into favoring one law of Moses over others, he gives them two nutshells:

> Then one of them, a lawyer, asked Him a question, testing Him, and saying, "Teacher, which is the great commandment in the law?"
>
> Jesus said to him, "'You shall love the Lord your God with all your heart, with all your soul, and with all your mind.' This is the first and great commandment. And the second is like it: 'You shall love your neighbor as yourself.' On these two commandments hang all the Law and the Prophets." (Matt. 22:35–40)

Jesus quotes Deuteronomy 6:5 and Leviticus 19:18, which I call *nutshells* because they include in themselves all God's law. How do we know how to love God and our neighbor? The rest of the Bible spells it out in precepts and proverbs, prayers and prophecies, examples and counterexamples, laments and love songs. Later, when Jesus gives his new commandment in the upper room, he gives it in shorthand: "A new commandment I give to you, that you love one another; as I have loved you, that you also love one another" (John 13:34). How do we learn to love each other as Jesus has loved us? We spend our lives reflecting on the Gospels and the apostolic teaching about the life and love of Jesus and, by the Spirit, work his love into our lives.

Paul's simple statements in Romans 8:6 are also nutshells. Much more than bare facts, these few words unfold in cascading implications. "To be carnally minded is death" is a sober warning, and the Bible displays carnal mindedness in living color from Adam and Eve to the Great Babylon of Revelation 18. And from the beginning, *death* has been the one-word summary of the fullest curse of God, pronounced in Genesis 2:17, then expounded and portrayed through the rest of Scripture.

But our attention is on Paul's summary blessing: "To be spiritually minded is life and peace." We've spent ten chapters exploring the implications of his charge to set our minds on things of the Spirit, what it means to devote our minds to our Beloved Christ. What remains is to look closely at Paul's multilayered incentive to spiritual mindedness, the promise of *life* and *peace*, two words that epitomize all that God promises, all that we could want and hope for, all that we find in him—*all his kingdom's joy.*

The Promised Life and Peace

We need to make a distinction. Our justification in Christ brings life and peace (Rom. 5:1, 10–11, 17–18), but this is not the life and peace God promises to the spiritually minded. Jesus said, "He who hears My word and believes in Him who sent Me has everlasting life, and shall not come into judgment, but has passed from death into life" (John 5:24). This justification that brings life and peace comes by faith (Rom. 1:17; 4:13); it is an "act of God's free grace," a one-time, all-or-nothing event[1]; it isn't worked in us by our minds being in step with the Spirit; it doesn't increase or decrease; we are either justified or not, spiritually alive or not, at peace with God and adopted into his

---

1. See Westminster Shorter Catechism, question and answer 33.

family or not. When God justifies us, he puts his Spirit in us, the Spirit of Life (Rom. 8:2). Again, this is not the greater life and peace promised to the spiritually minded.

Yet, as we saw at the beginning of this book, this new life and the Spirit's living in us are the fountain of spiritual mindedness. Without justification and the Spirit there would be no sanctification.[2] And this sanctification is the life of the Spirit, for we are raised with Christ to "walk in newness of life" (Rom. 6:4). In this new life, God's "divine power has given to us all things that pertain to life and godliness" (2 Peter 1:3). In this new life, the Spirit transforms all the powers of our soul, but the renewed mind is a kind of firstfruits of that new life. The spiritual mind feeds and stirs the affections, restrains wandering appetites, trains the conscience, communes with Christ, draws close to God, rejects the world. This is the life of sanctification by God's grace, and when our minds are on the Spirit, his life flourishes in us.

Beyond this, spiritual mindedness brings a richness of life (John 10:10). When Paul tells the Thessalonians, "Now we live, if you stand fast in the Lord" (1 Thess. 3:8), he means that he's been comforted by Timothy's report of their spiritual thriving (vv. 6–7), and such comfort enriches life. We feel "life" in this elevated sense when our children follow Christ (3 John 4), when we stand before God's sublime beauty in nature, or even in the darkest valleys of life, when friends refuse to desert us. God created us with a capacity not just to survive but to thrive—to find comfort and satisfaction and delight. The promise of life and peace to the spiritual mind is a joyous life, an abundant life, a life worth living.

This life worth living necessarily includes the peace promised to the spiritual mind. Again, this isn't the absolute peace

2. Justification and sanctification are two benefits of our redemption in Christ and cannot be separated. As John Calvin put it, "There is no justification without sanctification, no forgiveness without renewal of life, no real faith from which the fruits of new obedience do not grow" (*Institutes*, 3.1.16).

with God that we have by being reconciled to him in Jesus Christ (Rom. 5:1). Yes, the peace of justification liberates our minds before God and prepares us to enjoy him. But the peace promised to the spiritual mind is the fruit of God's Spirit in us; it composes us in hardship, temptations, and all the troubles of this world that threaten to fill us with fear, discouragement, and anxiety. Such peace maintains our souls in strength and, through the love of Christ in the gospel, keeps fear from overwhelming us.

How Does Spiritual Mindedness Bring Life and Peace?

Christ gives those who believe in him abundant life and peace that passes understanding. From the day of our new birth in him until the day we die, a principal way he conveys that life and peace to us is through our growth in spiritual mindedness. This is the promise of Romans 8:6. And as we think about how Christ communicates that life and peace to us, we find that it's inseparable from God's love.

Spiritual Mindedness Keeps Fresh Our Sense of God's Love

Knowing that God loves us is the only reliable, lasting comfort and refreshment in life. His love is constant and unquenchable, but our assurance and awareness of it can ebb. When David lost confidence in God's love, he moved toward God and prayed, "Restore to me the joy of Your salvation" (Ps. 51:12). The way we stay sure of anyone's love is by drawing close, connecting our minds and hearts in personal communion. That's spiritual mindedness: fixing our thoughts on God as he is revealed in Christ, drawing close, communing with him. That prepares us to receive his expressions of love through his Word and Spirit. It tunes us to the frequency of his love.

We especially keep a sense of God's love by remembering. We call to mind God's pledges of his favor on us in Christ, as well as his demonstrations of that favor in Scripture and through our lives. Asaph did this when he was tempted to think that God had abandoned him:

> Will the Lord cast off forever?
> And will He be favorable no more?
> Has His mercy ceased forever?
> Has His promise failed forevermore?
> Has God forgotten to be gracious?
> Has He in anger shut up His tender mercies? *Selah*
>
> And I said, "This is my anguish;
> But I will remember the years of the right hand of the
>   Most High."
> I will remember the works of the LORD;
> Surely I will remember Your wonders of old.
> I will also meditate on all Your work,
> And talk of Your deeds.
> Your way, O God, is in the sanctuary;
> Who is so great a God as our God?
> You are the God who does wonders;
> You have declared Your strength among the peoples.
> You have with Your arm redeemed Your people,
> The sons of Jacob and Joseph. *Selah* (Ps. 77:7–15)

Spiritual Mindedness Teaches Us to Cherish God's Love

Just as jewelers assess the value of a pearl by close inspection, when we meditate on the nature and quality of God's love in Christ, we see its perfections, its luster, its glory. We note how the patience of his love suffers long, enduring the weakness of our flesh and our wandering, and how the wisdom of his love overcomes the obstacles of Satan's hatred and the world's seduction. We marvel that the generosity of his love overflows in tender reassurances and precious promises in his Word. We are dazzled by the condescending selflessness of his love that shines in his humbling himself to become man to suffer and die for us. We can't deny his desire to be with us in his sending his Spirit to live in us. By such reflection, the spiritual mind learns the priceless value of God's love and cherishes it as the marrow of life.

Spiritual Mindedness Teaches Us How to Feed on God's Love in His Means of Grace

Immediately after God sent his Spirit at Pentecost, he showed us how he daily feeds and strengthens his people: "And they devoted themselves to the apostles' teaching and the fellowship, to the breaking of bread and the prayers" (Acts 2:42 ESV). The apostles' teaching is the Word of God, the fellowship is our mutual building up of each other with our gifts of the Spirit, the breaking of bread is the Lord's Supper, and the prayers are our corporate prayers by the Spirit of supplication (Zech. 12:10). We call these the ordinary means of grace, and by them the Spirit instructs us, corrects us, encourages us, trains us—in short, he gives us all we need for life and godliness, all that Christ secured for us in our redemption. The spiritually minded are alert to these means; they know this is how God feeds our spirits, they study how to find God's love in them, and they come to the table.

Spiritual Mindedness Keeps Our Loves in Order

Because it teaches us the value of God's love and how to feed on it, spiritual mindedness trains our hearts to love God above all and to love all things in their right relation to God. When our loves are in order and God is our all in all, we aren't beguiled by the world or our flesh. We grow into the balance of affections God intended when he made us, so that our love for his creation feeds our love for him and doesn't compete with it. But when our love is disordered, we're overcome by frustration, anger, and anxiety and cannot be content. Peace is impossible.

Spiritual Mindedness Keeps Our Hearts Primed for All Service to the Beloved

Our Beloved assures us, "If you keep My commandments, you will abide in My love, just as I have kept My Father's commandments and abide in His love. . . . You are My friends if you do whatever I command you" (John 15:10, 14). Life and peace will not persist, much less thrive and flourish, if we neglect the offices of love to Christ.

Spiritual mindedness fights off the enemies of our love and faithfulness. It fights off distraction by fixing our attention on "those things which are above, where Christ is, sitting at the right hand of God" (Col. 3:1). It wards off despondency due to guilt and shame by returning us daily to the cross and those innumerable assurances of God's love and forgiveness in Christ. When we are tempted to "grow weary of doing good" (Gal. 6:9 ESV), spiritual mindedness reinvigorates us with delight in God's love. And because spiritual mindedness keeps us feeding on God's grace in his ordinary means, we're prepared for action (1 Peter 1:13), equipped and eager to serve our Beloved. Life and peace don't languish under the care of the spiritual mind; they prosper by the promises of our Beloved.

As great as all these are, they are but the fringe benefits.

Heaven on Earth?

We were made for this ultimate purpose: to see God in Christ and by seeing him to know happiness and be like him. Because God in his eternal and unchangeable perfection is all blessedness, our sight of him in heaven will render us blessed to the as-yet-unimaginable limits of our capacity as creatures. This is *all His kingdom's joy*: God himself. By now you can see that spiritual mindedness lifts us into the closest approach to that beatific vision that faith is capable of. Faith is not sight, so even in raptures of communion with Christ now we will always feel the unease that something is missing, something is even unattainable—for now.

A day is coming when "faith shall be sight, the clouds be rolled back as a scroll."[3] Until then, "we walk by faith, not by sight" (2 Cor. 5:7). By the Spirit, that faith transports us into the presence of our Beloved, where there is life and peace.

Reflection and Praxis

1. For each of the subsections describing how spiritual mindedness brings life and peace, assess where you are in your maturity:

- What do you do each day to keep a fresh sense of God's love?
- How do you keep a sense of the high value of God's love?
- Do you treat the means of grace as ways to receive God's love (and everything else he promises in them)?
- How do you keep your love for God and created things in proper order?
- Does your devotional life keep you from the distractions, despondency, weariness, and laxity that undermine communion with God and chip away at your life and peace?

2. At the end of the introduction, I asked what ideas you already had about spiritual mindedness. Have your ideas changed as you worked through this book? If so, how?

3. Horatio G. Spafford, "It Is Well with My Soul," 1873.

3. In light of this study, do you think of yourself as growing in spiritual mindedness? Explain your answer.

4. At the end of the introduction, I asked what you would like God to do in your life as you read this book and to write a brief prayer seeking his grace for that. Look back at your prayer. How has God begun to answer your prayer?

Suggestions for Further Reading

Michael Allen's *Grounded in Heaven: Recentering Christian Hope and Life on God* (Grand Rapids: Eerdmans, 2018) helps us better understand the role of the beatific vision in life, while Hans Boersma's *Seeing God: The Beatific Vision in Christian Tradition* (Grand Rapids, 2018) is a deep and detailed history of that doctrine.

acknowledgments

God kindly provided many saints to help me write this book.

The spark came in November of 2020, when out of the blue Dave Almack from P&R asked me whether I'd be interested in any new writing projects—even though it had been twenty years since my last book. Thanks, Dave, for the timely interest and encouragement.

Eric Manthei was my faithful first responder: I could send him a chapter or a paragraph or a new title idea to get a quick and frank reaction, and he delivered without fail and without complaint. After Eric helped me knock off the rough edges, I had a wave of readers and reactors to help me further refine the manuscript: Julie Brister, Joshua Butcher, Jesse Carnes, Tom Courtney, Jonathan and Emma Davis, Chris Finnegan, Bob Hardister, Matt Hurley, Landy and Robin Ligon, Paula Lundgaard, Dagan Mayfield, Jessica McDonald, Barbara Mes, Peggy Mills, John Pickett, Kathleen Pourciau, Randy Scott, Geoff Smith, Matt Thomas, and Chip Ueltschey. Some read a few chapters, some read the whole kit and caboodle. Some cheered me on, some sobered me up. All made me think. May God reward each of you for your kindness to me.

Amanda Martin and Cheryl Molin at P&R helped to put the finishing touches on the manuscript, and readers will, without knowing it, benefit from their keen attention to detail.

I knew John Holberg before he was a legend in the library at Covenant College. When I asked him to help me find an obscure journal article, he not only delivered the article I wanted but pointed me to the article I needed instead. Your legend title is justified, John.

My old friends John Pickett and George Reiswig each lent their expertise where I lacked it and gave my two favorite illustrations the ring of truth.

We met Lenka Slobodová (now Knoetze) when we first moved to Slovakia with MTW. She later moved to South Africa to work as an illustrator and graphic designer with Operation Mobilization. When I asked her to draw the cruciform tree that Willa Cather described, I wasn't prepared for how strikingly she would capture it. Lenka, you have my admiration and gratitude.

My wife, Paula, has always been my closest, most detailed proofreader. Her role expanded this time to work as a substitute teacher, senior caregiver, and church office administrator, enabling me to take a leave of absence to write. In other words, there would be no book without her. I love you, P.

God is good.

Also by Kris Lundgaard

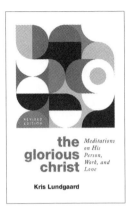

Become more like Christ by meditating on his beauty. Originally published as *Through the Looking Glass*, this revised devotional work brings the wisdom of Puritan John Owen to a broad audience.

This revised edition of Kris Lundgaard's best-selling classic brings the wisdom of Puritan John Owen to a broad audience. Find insight, encouragement, and hope for your battle with sin.

"This is a precious book . . . because of its vivid focus on Jesus and his glory . . . because of its piercing analysis of what goes wrong in Christian hearts and what to do about it . . . It is a fresh-flavored, doctrinal devotional of classic quality, which I enthusiastically recommend."
—**J. I. Packer**, Author, *Knowing God*

"Kris Lundgaard has done the impossible. He has given us some of the best of Puritan theology in a language all of us can understand. This book will challenge you to radical spiritual transformation!"
—**Richard L. Pratt Jr.**, President, Third Millennium Ministries

Also from P&R Publishing on Spiritual Growth

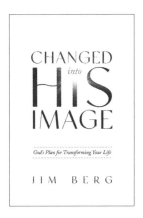

In this roadmap to spiritual growth, biblical counselor Jim Berg guides new and mature believers alike to better cultivate a deep relationship with Christ and respond wisely to God's direction for life.

"Dr. Jim Berg is one of the best communicators of God's truths in the church today. *Changed into His Image* is an indispensable discipleship resource that teaches Christians how to understand and kill sin, renew their minds, and behold Jesus. As they learn this, it will allow them to image Christ and magnify his name. Jim has been an invaluable teacher in my life, and this book is one that I love and use with those I counsel and mentor, as well as myself. It is a treasure to God's children."

—**Melli Dionne**, Biblical Counselor, Faith Biblical Counseling Ministries, Spokane, Washington; Author, *James and His Weird Mad*

Also from P&R Publishing on Spiritual Growth

Do you know who you are? In this Scripture-saturated devotional, pastor and biblical counselor Paul Tautges provides 90 meditations on your complete identity before God in Christ as saint, sinner, and sufferer. Day by day, center your thoughts and affections on the Savior and stay on God's good path as you live in a broken world.

"Paul explains how understanding our position in Christ . . . gives meaning and power to our struggle against sin and perseverance through suffering. This excellent volume is must-reading for anyone who feels they need help in becoming the person Jesus wants them to be."
—**Joni Eareckson Tada,** Founder, Joni and Friends International Disability Center

"[A] lovely series of meditations. . . . You will learn who you are in Jesus Christ, you will learn how he provides all that you truly need, and you will learn why it is fitting that you submit to his good and perfect will. . . . This is a book that blessed me and one I am certain will bless you as well."
—**Tim Challies,** Blogger, www.challies.com

Did you find this book helpful?
Consider writing a review online.
We appreciate your feedback!

Or write to P&R at editorial@prpbooks.com
with your comments. We'd love to hear from you.